JR L N mella

# BIBLE CLASS COMMENTARY

# BIBLE CLASS COMMENTARY

## 1 & 2 THESSALONIANS
## 1 & 2 TIMOTHY

Henry T. Mahan

 EVANGELICAL PRESS

EVANGELICAL PRESS
16-18 High Street, Welwyn, Herts., AL6 9EQ, England.

© Evangelical Press 1984

*First published 1984*

ISBN 0 85234 185 7

Cover picture by kind permission of Rev. R. Simpson

Typeset in Great Britain by
Beaver ReproGraphics, Watford, Hertfordshire.
Printed by Anchor Brendon Ltd., Tiptree, Essex, England.

# CONTENTS

# 1 THESSALONIANS

# Evidences of our election

## 1 Thessalonians 1:1-10

Paul and Silas came to Thessalonica after they left Philippi and preached there for at least three weeks (Acts 17:1-4). The foundation of this church was then laid. Timothy came back later, establishing and comforting the young converts and returning to Paul with the good news of their faith and love. Paul wrote this, said to be his first epistle, about the year A.D. 51.

*v.1.* The salutation from Paul, Silas and Timothy to the church at Thessalonica is sent with his usual prayer: **'Grace be to you and peace from the Father and the Son.'**

*v.2.* The apostle gives thanks for every member of the church, Jew and Gentile, rich and poor, leaders and followers. He does not ascribe anything to their free will or decision, nor does he ascribe anything to himself or his companions, who preached the gospel to them; but he gives thanks and glory to God alone, assuring them of his prayers for them (2 Thess. 2:13; 1 Sam.12:23). **'I am mindful of you in prayer.'**

*v.3.* **'I constantly remember'** with thanksgiving before God
1. **'Your work**, energized and activated by your **faith.'** True faith is a working grace. Faith that does not produce good works and obedience is not saving faith (James 2:14-20).
2. **'Your labours**, motivated by **love!'** Love to Christ and to one another will engage a believer in worship, prayer and in ministering cheerfully to the needs of others. Labours and

works motivated by anything but love are not pleasing to God.

*v.4.* **'My brethren'** (this is the relationship of those in the family of God) (Mark 3:31-35), beloved of God and beloved of me. **'I know that God has elected,** chosen and fore-ordained you to eternal life.' This is not an election to office or service, but to *salvation* (Eph. 1:3, 4; Rom. 9:10-16).

Paul gives many evidences why he knows they have been chosen to salvation in Christ.

*v.5.*    1. 'The manner in which the gospel came to you reveals your election,' not merely in the external ministry of it, but in the internal efficacy of it through the power and revelation of God's Holy Spirit. There is a difference in hearing the arguments and teaching of men and in hearing the Word preached and made clear to the heart by the Spirit of God (1 Cor. 2:4, 5, 9, 10; Matt. 16:13-17). 'This word of grace, which the Holy Spirit applied to your hearts, brought great conviction, blessed assurance of your interest in Christ and confidence in us as the ministers of Christ.'

*v.6.*    2. 'Another evidence of your election of God is the fact that you received that gospel and became followers of the Lord.' We do not emulate or follow any man as such, but we follow the leadership, instruction, example and correction of those whom God sends to minister to us the gospel (Heb. 13:7). Babes in Christ need to listen to elders and follow them as they follow Christ.
    3. 'Also, you received the Word and stood for the gospel in spite of the afflictions and persecutions brought upon you for your faith' (Acts 17:5-9). True saving faith clings to Christ and his Word, regardless of the consequences caused by that faith.

*v.7.*    4. 'Another evidence of your election is that you, by your faith, works and love, became examples and patterns for all believers!' Though young in faith, they set an example for others – examples in worship, faithfulness, holiness, conversation and conduct.

*v.8.* 5. 'You became witnesses, evangelists and missionaries.' A person who has been chosen to salvation and brought to a living, vital union with Christ will carry a great burden for all people (Rom. 10:1; 9:1-3). He will witness to others and cheerfully support those who preach the gospel.

*v.9.* 6. 'You turned from your idols to love and serve God, who lives and is the true God.' We turn from our internal idols (of pride, self-love, lusts, ambition and rebellion) to submit to his will and providence. We turn from our external idols, not only of false ideas of God and religious ceremonies, but from materialism, family and other earthly ties, and all things and persons which hinder our walk with him!

*v.10.* 7. 'You look forward to and await the return of our Lord Jesus Christ, who died for our sins, was raised from the dead and is seated at the Father's right hand. He will come again; you believe this and await his coming' (John 14:3; Acts 1:10, 11).

# Evidences of ministerial sincerity

## 1 Thessalonians 2:1-8

The apostle, giving an account of his successful ministry among the Thessalonians, commends their readiness to receive the gospel.

*v.1.* What a comfort it is to a minister of the gospel to have his own conscience and the witness of others declare that he has been true to the gospel of God's glory, true to those who have heard him and that he has not run nor laboured in vain! What an encouragement to see that God has brought forth fruit from the Word preached! (Acts 20:20, 21, 26, 27.) If a false prophet is known by the fruits of his ministry, may not a true minister be known by his? (Matt. 7:15, 16.)

*v.2.* Paul was put in prison and shamefully treated at Philippi (Acts 16). He was not discouraged nor turned from his purpose to make Christ known; but as soon as he came to Thessalonica, he preached Christ as boldly as ever, meeting with much contention and opposition. Persecution and opposition ought to encourage rather than discourage us, for we are faithfully warned by our Lord that the natural man and the religionist will not receive the gospel of the grace of God! (John 16:1-4). But **'we earnestly contend'**, also, and this may be the main point here.

*v.3.* 'We are willing to be a bit contentious and appeal to you with great zeal and fervour, for our preaching of the gospel of Christ does not originate from error, delusion or an improper motive (nor in fraud or deceit). Our design is not to win you to ourselves, to a party or to glory in your flesh, but that you may *know Christ*.' Paul had no secular aims or goals, but was in reality what he professed to be. In the next verses he gives the reasons and evidences of his sincerity!

*v.4.* 1. 'We are *stewards* of God, entrusted with the gospel.' It is required of a steward that he be faithful. The gospel he preached was not his own, but was the gospel of God (1 Cor. 9:16). We shall give an account of our ministry (Heb. 13:17).

2. 'Our design was to *please God*, not to please men.' The gospel of Christ must not be compromised and accommodated

to the thoughts, desires and fancies of men, but it is designed to mortify the flesh and glorify the grace and mercy of God in Christ.

*v.5.*   3. 'We *avoided flattery* and praising of the flesh, for we were determined to preach Christ, not to gain an interest in the affection of men. We did not flatter men to gain their support nor their interest in the gospel.' Our weapons are not carnal (2 Cor. 10:4, 5).

4. 'We *avoided covetousness*. We did not use the ministry as a cloak or a covering to hide a covetous and greedy motive. Our design was not to enrich ourselves through preaching (2 Peter 2:3). God always met our needs and provided our living, regardless of what men thought of us.'

*v.6.*   5. ' We *avoided ambition and vain glory.*' Paul did not covet their praise, nor to be called 'rabbi,' nor to be adored by them. He was not seeking honour from men, but that honour which comes from God (John 5:44). He was certainly an apostle and worthy of respect and double honour. He could have used his authority as an apostle and demanded esteem and special care, but he wanted nothing to hinder their coming to faith in Christ.

*v.7.*   6. 'We were *gentle* among you.' Such kindness, gentleness and patience are becoming to the gospel of Christ and recommend the grace of God, for he is kind and gentle in dealing with sinners (Eph. 4:32). Though Paul did not flatter the flesh, he was kind and condescending to all men and became all things to all men. He showed the kindness and care of a mother nursing and cherishing her own children. The Word of God is indeed powerful and it comes often with awesome authority upon the minds of men, but it is not our place as faulty men to use this Word harshly nor in a rude, cruel and overbearing manner (2 Tim. 2:24, 25).

*v.8.*   The apostle had such a strong affection for these

people that he was not only willing to preach the gospel to
them but was willing to give his life for them; they had
become so dear to him.

# We have these things in common

## 1 Thessalonians 2:9-20

Paul continues his account of his ministry among the
Thessalonians by expressing his deep personal regard for
them and his thanksgiving to God for them, encouraging
them in their faith, their trials and their afflictions for the
sake of the gospel.

*vv. 9, 10.*    The Scripture is very clear on the matter of
support and material care for those who preach the
gospel as pastors, missionaries and evangelists (1 Cor.
9:11-14; Gal. 6:6). But when Paul was among these
people, he worked as a tent-maker (Acts 18:3), which proves
that he was not seeking material gain and did not use the
ministry for a cloak of covetousness. In his life, conduct and
conversation he put forth every effort to keep from bringing
reproach on Christ or hindering the gospel. People watch us
and listen to us, often in a critical fashion, in order that they
may find some reason not to believe our gospel. Let us avoid
every appearance of evil and inconsistency which might give
them cause to accuse us of hypocrisy!

*vv. 11, 12.*    He reminds them of his tenderness, compassion
and faithfulness in ministering to them, exhorting them also to
walk in a manner of life that is worthy of their holy calling.
We are in this world, but not of this world! (Phil. 3:17-21;
1 Cor. 7:29-31.)

*v. 13.*    This is perhaps the greatest compliment Paul could pay them and the greatest blessing that could come their way. Paul, without ceasing, praises God that it is true of them. They heard the gospel of Christ from Paul, but they did not only hear Paul, but God, and they received the gospel of God's glory not in the words, tradition and logic of a mere man, but they received it as the Word of God (1 Thess. 1:5). God works by his Word, and when the Word is heard in power, as the Word of God, it works effectually to the bringing to life of dead sinners and the enlightening of dark minds! Men need to cease from arguing against Scripture and to hear the Word of the Lord with the heart in faith and submission.


*vv. 14, 15,*    Wherever you find the children of God (whether in Judea, Thessalonica, Europe or America), they have most things in common!

1. They agree on the depravity, inability and sinfulness of the flesh.

2. They ascribe all the glory for salvation and providence to God alone.

3. They rest in the person and work of Christ alone for all things.

4. Their only rule for faith and conduct is the Word of God.

5. Christ is the object of faith, the glory of God their object in life.

6. They endure persecution and ridicule from a world of unbelievers, both in religion and in the world (John 15:18, 19;16:1, 2; 1 Peter 4:12-14).


*v. 16.*    The enemies of Christ and of his gospel did all that they could to keep Paul from preaching the gospel to the Gentiles. The Jews called for the death of Christ, killed their own prophets and persecuted Paul, holding to their own self-righteousness and doctrine of works. They are the enemies of all men. But the wrath of God has come upon them

completely and for ever. Zealous religionists who deny the free
grace of God are special objects of God's wrath (2 Thess. 2:
10-12; 2 Peter 3:16).

*vv. 17, 18.*    In these verses Paul apologizes for having to leave
them after such a short ministry. He was forced to leave by the
rage of his persecutors. He had determined to return but was
hindered by Satan, the great enemy of the gospel, who stirred
up opposition and contention. Paul was absent from them in
body, but not in heart.

*vv. 19, 20.*    These believers in Christ Paul calls his hope, his
joy, his crown of rejoicing and his glory in the presence of the
Lord Jesus at his coming.
    1. They were his **'hope'** and **'joy'**. He had great hope for
them and their conversion was a matter of joy for him now
and would be at the return of Christ.
    2. They were his **'crown of rejoicing'**, or his victor's wreath
of triumph. They would be trophies of God's grace and Paul
would rejoice, encircled by these to whom he had preached
the gospel.
    3. They were his **'glory'** and **'joy'**. Believers never glory in
men, but in the mercy and grace of God in Christ towards
men! These believers were fruits of his ministry also, and
therefore brought hope, rejoicing and joy to his heart.


# Comfort in Tribulation

## 1 Thessalonians 3:1-13

Paul gives an account of his sending Timothy to Thessalonica
to minister to them. He expresses his joy over the report
Timothy brought back concerning their faith and love.

*vv. 1, 2.*    Paul had a great love for the people in this church, and he is saying that when the suspense and yearning for some word from them became unbearable he was content to remain alone in Athens and send Timothy to them.

1. **'To establish you.'** These people were young converts and needed to be established in the truth of the gospel. This is done by the ministry of the Word (Rom. 16:25; Eph. 4:11-14).

2. **'To comfort you concerning your faith.'** It is the will of God that his people have assurance, peace and comfort in Christ. These people had been persecuted and afflicted because of their faith. Paul intended that they understand that their faith was like precious faith with (the same precious faith as) the apostles, and they should stand fast and be comforted in that faith (2 Peter 1:1).

*v. 3.*    'None of you should be surprised, disturbed or led astray by trials and afflictions for the sake of the gospel, for you know that trials are the appointed lot of all of God's people--they are appointed by God!' It is the will of God that we should have them, patiently bearing them and profiting by them (John 16:1-3; James 1:2, 3; 1 Thess. 5:18).

*v. 4.*    'When I was there in person I told you that you would suffer tribulation, and it has come to pass' (Acts 17:5-9). The apostle did not deceive people with promises of worldly prosperity, good health, fame and ease in this world; on the contrary, he told them, as our Master told his disciples, that they would have trouble in the flesh (John 16:33).

*v. 5.*    'This is one of the reasons why I sent Timothy to you, that I might know if your faith is staggering under these afflictions or standing firm.' The apostle speaks of his fear that Satan may tempt them to turn back and his preaching among them prove to be in vain (Heb. 10:32-39).

*vv.6, 7.*    Timothy brought back a good report! It is always a great joy to preachers and all believers to know that the people of God in any location continue in the faith and love of Christ (3 John 4). These two graces are always found together: faith and love. It is impossible to separate them. Those who believe, love! Therefore, in spite of all the trials and pressures of his own ministry, Paul was comforted by their faith.

*vv.8, 9.*    Paul carried about with him a sentence of death, being hunted, imprisoned and sentenced, but he says now, upon the news of their faith and love, his spirit is revived and he really lives! He had given thanks to God for them (1 Thess. 1:2; 3) and now, having received a further account of their faith growing under trying circumstances, he must give fresh thanks to God!

*vv.10-13.*    Here is an account of the prayer Paul prayed continually:
  1. That he might visit them again.
  2. That he might minister the Word to them and more perfectly instruct them in the knowledge of divine things. The ministry of the Word is the means of planting faith, increasing faith and perfecting it. There is no believer living who does not need the continued preaching, teaching and reading of the Word that he might grow in grace and the knowledge of Christ (1 Cor. 8:2; 3:18; 13:9, 12).
  3. 'If I come to you, God himself must guide and direct my way.' A journey is not to be taken without the will of God — dependence on his will, seeking his will and submission to his will. Men may devise their ways, but God directs their goings! (James 4:13-15; Rom. 1:10.)
  4. 'The Lord make you to abound in love towards one another and towards all men, as our love abounds towards you.'
  5. 'That God may establish your hearts in holiness before him.' This is where the true work of repentance, faith and sanctification is performed — in the heart before God. The Lord Jesus will come and his saints with him; then the excel-

lency of heart-holiness, as well as the necessity of it, will appear.

# A holy walk pleases God

## 1 Thessalonians 4:1-12

Paul exhorts the Thessalonians in their daily walk and conduct to seek to please the Lord. Particularly, he urges sexual purity, brotherly love, peaceful living and self-supporting labour!

*vv.1-3.* Paul does not threaten, badger and condemn these brethren in his plea for godliness and holiness of life, but he uses words like 'I beg of you', 'I request and admonish you' to do these things. He gives four reasons for holy living:

1. **'By the Lord Jesus'** — by virtue of your union with Jesus Christ. We are not our own, but we are bought with a price. We belong to Christ and by his mercy we are one with Christ. We are children of God, therefore, we ought to walk as he walked.

2. **'You have received of us how you ought to walk.'** The inspired apostles have given us the Scriptures, which are perfectly clear on the matter of our conduct and behaviour.

3. **'To please God.'** Our motive and objective is not to please and gratify ourselves, nor men, but to please *God* — to glorify him and to do his will. 'Lord, what would *you* have me do?'

4. **'This is the will of God'** — that you be consecrated, separated and set apart from the world, that you grow in grace in the knowledge of Christ, and that you **'abound more and more'** (that you attain greater spiritual maturity).

*vv.3-5.*    'That you abstain from fornication' — from all sexual impurity. Fornication is especially mentioned because this sin was common among the Gentiles and not considered to be sin by them. Most translations render it, 'that you abstain from all sexual vice' and immorality, such as adultery, incest, homosexuality and the like.

'That every one of you should know how to control and manage his own body in purity and consecration.' Many writers say the words, 'his vessel', mean his wife (1 Peter 3:7; 1 Cor. 7:2-5).

One's body is not to be given over to the gratification of passions and cravings as are those of the heathen who know not God.

*v.6.*    This verse is commonly understood as against defrauding and cheating others in business, trade and measures — against taking advantage of the weak and ignorant (and can be thus used, for such conduct is not of God). But the subject here is not business nor trade; it is sexual purity. We believers are exhorted to treat one another's marriages and partners as we want others to deal with us. Do not covet or desire another's wife, thereby defrauding him.

*v.7.*    God has not called us to take part in any of the unholy practices related above, but our calling is to holiness in thought, looks, words and in action.

*v.8.*    Therefore whoever disregards, sets aside and rejects these principles and words is not disregarding and rejecting the words and will of a mere man, but is in reality rejecting and disregarding the very will of God himself. We know this, for God has given us his Holy Spirit to convince us of sin and righteousness. His Spirit in us clearly convinces us of his will in these matters, and we need no other argument.

*vv.9, 10.*    'Now concerning your love for one another, you have no need for anyone to write to you and encourage you to love one another, for you have been personally taught of

God to love one another (John 13:34, 35; 1 John 4:7-12).
Let this love increase more and more!'

*vv.11, 12.* **'Study to be quiet'.** Make it your ambition and
goal to live peaceably in your homes, church and businesses, to
cause no disturbance and turmoil by tale-bearing, gossiping
and unkind words or accusations.

**'Do your own business.'** Mind your own affairs. Do not
concern yourself with the business and private lives of others
except when you are asked to do so. Take care of your own
calling and ministry; use your gifts as God enables you and
pray for others to be used in theirs.

**'Work with your own hands.'** There were some who would
not work at all but expected to live off the charity of others
(2 Thess. 3:10-13).

**'Walk honestly and honourably before people outside the
church,'** so as to have their respect. Be self-supporting. Do not
depend on those who are without Christ to support the church
of the Lord Jesus or the family of God.

# The believer's comfort regarding death

## 1 Thessalonians 4:13-18

The apostle comforts the Thessalonians who grieve because of
the death of their friends and relatives who died in the faith
of Christ. His design is to persuade them from excessive sorrow
and grief (which are unbecoming for a believer), to assure them
of the coming of the Lord and the resurrection of all believers
and to comfort them with these words of promise and
instruction.

*v.13.*    There are many things about death, life after death
and eternity of which we will remain ignorant until it comes
to our time to die. But there are some things concerning those
who die in the Lord of which we need not, and ought not, to
be ignorant. If these things are really understood and considered, our sorrows and grief will be reduced.

Sorrow and grief are not unlawful, but natural. We weep
for ourselves when we are deprived of their presence, and we
weep for our temporary loss, though it be their eternal gain,
but our sorrow is not like that of the unbeliever who has no
hope of eternal life, or of seeing these loved ones again. They
have every reason to be totally grief-stricken, but we do not,
for death is only a temporary separation for us.

*v.14.*    'We believe that our Lord died and rose again.' Every
believer knows this to be true. This is fundamental to our
faith (1 Cor. 15:12-22).

Therefore, those who have died in the faith of Christ will
be raised also. They were chosen in Christ, crucified with
Christ, raised and seated with him in the heavenlies. Having
left this world, they are with him in paradise and will return
with him when he comes again. The believer cannot be separated from Christ (John 17:23, 24). What sort of body or
dwelling they have now, we do not know (2 Cor. 5:1-4); but
we know that when our bodies are raised, we shall be like
Christ (1 John 3:1, 2; Luke 24:36-43).

*v.15.*    'We declare unto you by the Word of the Lord,
    '1. That Christ shall return to this earth (John 14:1-3;
Acts 1:9-11).
    '2. That we who are still alive on earth when Christ comes
shall not precede or go before those who are dead.' The dead
will rise and the living will be changed and we shall all go
together into the enjoyment of Christ (1 Cor. 15:50-53).

*v.16.*    'The Lord himself.' Not an angel, a messenger or a
representative.

'Shall descend from heaven.' He was on our earth and ascended into heaven after his resurrection. When all things are accomplished, he will descend from heaven into our air.

'With a shout.' It will not be a private, unknown, secret affair, but will be with the shout of a Conqueror, a King, and every eye shall see him.

'The voice of the archangel.' Perhaps one great angel will give notice of his return, but he will be accompanied by many angels (Jude 9; 2 Thess. 1:7).

'With the trump of God.' This will awaken all who sleep and summon the world to appear before him (1 Cor. 15:52).

'The dead in Christ will rise first' – before we who are living are changed and before the unsaved dead are raised (Rev. 20:5, 6).

*v.17.*   The dead will rise and the living will be changed into the likeness of Christ and we shall go up to meet the Lord in the air. At this time it is indicated that he does not descend to the earth. The earth is not fit to receive him, for it must be purged with fire, and there will be a new earth upon which he will descend and dwell with his saints. He will take us to glory above until the general conflagration and destruction of the world is over. But whatever (by the purpose and decree of God) takes place, we shall for ever be with the Lord.

*v.18.*   'Comfort one another with these words!'

1. When believers die, they do not cease to be, but they are asleep in Christ.

2. These who sleep in him will return for their bodies when he comes.

3. He will come with great power and glory and we shall, with those who are raised, meet him in the air.

4. We shall for ever be with the Lord. This is our comfort, our hope and our expectation.

# Looking for his return

## 1 Thessalonians 5:1-11

The apostle writes about the coming of the Lord — its sudden-
ness and the necessity of watchfulness on the part of believers.
He exhorts us concerning our duties and responsibilities to the
Lord and to one another and closes with a prayer for all
believers.

*v.1.*    To write to believers that Christ will come again (John
14:3; Acts 1:10, 11), that the dead will be raised and that
living believers will be changed into his likeness is necessary,
for this encourages our faith and hope. It comforts us when
we come to die or to bury loved ones and it encourages us in
trials. But to write about the *time* it will occur and the *season*
of the year it will take place is unnecessary, for (1) it would
be idle speculation to satisfy the curious; and (2) no man
knows that day, hour or season (Matt. 24:36). True believers
do not wish to know more than God is pleased to reveal.

*v.2.*    We do know that the return of Christ will be sudden
and unexpected, taking the world of unbelievers by surprise,
as a thief surprises those who are asleep (Luke 12:40).

*v.3.*    Unbelievers talk of peace and safety. They promise
themselves much ease, peace and good health for years to
come — then suddenly death, judgement and the coming of
the Lord are upon them, as in the days of Noah (Luke 17:
26, 27), as a woman carries a child in her womb and without
any warning or notice her labour begins. Careless, indifferent
unbelievers shall be overtaken and shall not escape.

*v.4.* The natural man's understanding is darkened with respect to the true knowledge of God, the nature of sin, the way of salvation by Christ, the return of Christ, eternal glory and eternal condemnation (Eph. 4:17-19). We have been called out of darkness and enlightened by the Holy Spirit. We are not in darkness, therefore we live in expectation, looking for his return (1 Thess. 1:9, 10).

*vv.5, 6.* He calls us children of light (2 Cor. 4:3-7). We are enlightened persons, whose understanding has been enlightened by the Holy Spirit concerning the person and work of Christ (Eph. 1:17-19). We are children of the gospel day, in distinction from the religious darkness. Therefore let us not be in a drowsy, indifferent frame of mind and spirit, like the unbeliever. Let us not be taken up with the cares and concerns of this world, but let us set a watch over our hearts, our faith and our fellowship, living as temporary citizens of this world. We are travellers passing through.

*vv.7, 8.* By 'sleep' and 'drunkenness' he does not mean natural sleep or drunkenness from wine, but a stupor of mind that forgets God and spiritual matters, giving itself to indulging carnal vices and materialism. These things come naturally to unbelievers, since they are children of darkness. But we, who are of the light of understanding and the day of revelation, are in a warfare, constantly on guard against evil within and without. The man who is provided with faith, hope and love will not be found wanting. The believer is pictured as a soldier, prepared to meet the enemy and prepared for his Lord's return!

*v.9.* The elect of God were not chosen in Christ to be destroyed by his wrath and judgement, but that we might obtain salvation through our Lord Jesus Christ (Eph. 1:3-5; Rom. 8:1; 2 Thess. 2:13).

*v.10.*   Christ died for us with this purpose in view: that he might make us partakers of his life. There is no reason why we should be in doubt of our salvation if we are in Christ by faith (Matt. 1:21). Whether we are alive when he comes or whether we are dead, we shall, because of his life and death, live forever with him.

*v.11.*   'Therefore, comfort one another, encourage one another, communicate to one another the things revealed to you. Edify, strengthen and build up one another in the faith of Christ.' This can be done by continual fellowship, worship, prayer, teaching and preaching, bearing one another's trials and sincere love.

# These final words

## 1 Thessalonians 5:12-28

*vv.12, 13.*   Paul speaks of faithful pastors and preachers. He exhorts the believers 'to know them'.
   1. 'Recognize, acknowledge, appreciate and respect them for what they are — the ministers of God!'
   2. 'Make yourselves known to them, converse freely with them, that they may know the state of your souls and speak a word in season.'
   3. 'Esteem or hold them in high and affectionate regard in appreciation of the work among you.'
   4. 'Be at peace among yourselves in regard to the ministry; do not find fault, disagree and take offence over trivial matters.' This makes the pastor's work more difficult and hinders the growth and unity of the church.
      a. **'They labour among you.'** No honour or respect is

due to the lazy, idle preachers who neglect prayer, study and
the ministry of the Word.

   b. '**They preside over you in the Lord**.' They are not
lords, but leaders and overseers of the church by the
authority of Christ.

   c. '**They admonish you**. They teach, warn, reprove and
exhort you in the things of the Lord,' and it is in this
respect that they are to be obeyed and followed (Heb.
13:7, 17).

*vv.14, 15.*    'I earnestly beseech you, according to our responsibility to the gospel, to the Lord, to one another and to the
testimony of the gospel:

'1. **Warn** and seriously advise them that are out of line in
doctrine, spirit and deed.' Unruly conduct and attitude are not
to be permitted to continue without warning and admonition.

'2. **Encourage** the weak.' Comfort those of a broken and
afflicted spirit. They have need of consolation and strength,
not rebuke!

'3. **Be patient** with everyone (even the unruly), always
keeping your temper, remembering your own infirmities and
afflictions' (Gal. 6:1). Be patient with everybody, even the
men of the world. It is only by God's grace that we walk in
the light!

4. Evil for evil is not the way of Christ. Getting even,
retaliating, seeking revenge is not for the believer. Rather,
*endure* injuries and misunderstandings with patience, show-
ing kindness towards all, and seeking the good of all, both in
the church and out.

*vv.16-18.*    I like to connect these three things:

   1. '**Rejoice evermore!**'
   2. '**Pray without ceasing!**'
   3. '**Give thanks to God in all things.**'

This is the will of God that we rejoice always, pray continually and give thanks. What we are, what we have, where
we are and all that happens in the life of a believer are the will

of God for us (Rom. 8:28). We should rejoice and give thanks!
Rejoice in prosperity or adversity. Pray always; live in an
attitude of prayer, even when you have no particular need
or request! Let your praise, prayer and thanksgiving constantly
rise to God. Very ungrateful is the man who does not set so
high a value on the righteousness of Christ and the hope of
eternal life that he allows anything in this life to overshadow
that gift of grace. How can I complain when I am an heir of
God and joint-heir with Christ?

*v.19.*    Paul does not mean the *person* of the Holy Spirit, who
works effectually as he will (John 3:8; 1 Cor. 12:11). He refers
to the *graces* of the Spirit, such as faith, love, joy, peace, etc.
He speaks of the *gifts* of the Spirit when they are neglected
and not put to use for the glory of God. To quench the Spirit
is to suppress or subdue his graces and gifts.

*v.20.*    Do not despise, make light of or be indifferent to the
message of those who preach and interpret the Word of God
(1 Cor. 14:3).

*v.21.*    Many in our day feel almost disgusted with the very
word 'preaching' because there are so many foolish and
ignorant persons giving out worthless sermons from the
pulpit. Therefore we must prove all words by the Scriptures
and hold fast to that which is good. Some people are critical
of everything; some embrace anything. The wise weigh all
things by the Word (1 John 4:1-3).

*v.22.*    I know that many interpret this as suggesting that we
avoid any conduct, behaviour, and actions that, while they
may not be wrong for us, yet they give the appearance of
wrong-doing. This is good advice, but not what the apostle is
talking about. He is speaking, as in the preceding verse, of
doctrinal evil! For example, when there is preaching, teaching
and interpretation of Scripture which, when tried by the
Word, does not appear to be false or wrong, but there is an

unhappy suspicion in the mind, a doubt or fear entertained,
and a concern that there is poison somewhere, then avoid it!
The truth of God is clear and gives glory to his name!

*vv.23, 24.*    Paul proceeds to pray for these believers. He prays
that the Lord God would, in a progressive manner, sanctify
them in spirit, soul and body. Calvin said, 'Our thoughts pure
and holy, our affections right and properly regulated and our
bodies dedicated to good work.' He prays that God would
keep them from falling away. He adds in verse 24, **'He will
do it.'** None of the sheep of Christ shall perish! (John 10:
27-29.)

*vv.25-28.*    **'Pray for us.'** Let every believer, especially God's
ministers, be the objects of our prayers. **'Greet one another
with a holy kiss.'** Be affectionate towards one another. 'Read
this epistle in the church. God be with you!'

# 2 THESSALONIANS

# Christ glorified in his saints

## 2 Thessalonians 1:1-12

*vv.1, 2.* '**Paul, Silas and Timothy, to the church of the Thessalonians in God and Christ.**' A true church is more than a group of people banded together for religious and social functions. A true church is the work and building of the Father in Christ. He chose us, adopts us, calls us, regenerates us and receives us in Christ (1 Cor. 1:30). A local church is a part of the great body of Christ — in God and in Christ (Eph. 5:25-32).

*v.3.* '**I give thanks to God for you, my brethren.**' All blessings come from God (James 1:17, 18). Therefore, '**it is meet**' (it is fitting) that we should give thanks to God, not only for the *presence* of faith and love but for the *growth* of it! Wherever the goodness of God is revealed, it is fitting for us to praise him. The welfare of our brethren ought to be so dear to us that we reckon their blessings to be our own.

*v.4.* '**We glory in you.**' We mention you with great rejoicing in the presence of other churches. Paul did not boast of their faith to shame other believers or to exalt his ministry, but to encourage other churches to imitate them.

He rejoiced in their patience and faith under great persecution and trial. Patience is the fruit and evidence of faith! There is nothing that will sustain us in trial but faith. The stronger our faith, the better we shall be able to endure trial and affliction. Failure under trial reveals unbelief or weakness of faith.

*vv.5, 6.* There is a twofold lesson here. God's righteous judgement is shown us as in a mirror.

1. The believer whose faith in Christ and love for the gospel bring upon him the wrath of the wicked (and this to try and prove his faith in the wisdom and purpose of God) will be exalted and glorified.

2. The wicked who prosper, who walk in pride and unbelief, having no fear of God's wrath, who mock and despise the grace of God, will be brought down (Deut. 32:35; Phil. 1:28; Ps. 73:12-22). God will set everything right, and justice will take place in his own time!

*v.7.* **'To you who are distressed and afflicted along with the rest of us.'** God had only one Son without sin, but none without suffering (2 Tim. 3:12-14; John 16:33). Christ will come from heaven as a Redeemer to his own people and as a Judge to the whole world. Paul represents the coming of Christ as one of horror and terror for all unbelievers. He will be accompanied by his mighty angels (the angels of his majesty), who will gather the elect and cast the wicked into hell (Matt. 13:41, 42; 24:31).

*v.8.* What is to be the nature of that fire we do not know, but flame and fire are often used in the Scriptures when the anger of God is spoken of. However, two things are noted here:

1. God will vindicate his elect (Luke 18:7). Vengeance is not ours, nor are we to desire it, but rather we are to desire the good of all. Vengeance belongs to God (Rom. 12:19; Heb. 10:30).

2. God will inflict vengeance with a view to his own glory, not only for our sake! This wrath will fall upon those who know not God and believe not the gospel of Christ (John 17:3). Ignorance of God and contempt for the gospel of his Son will bring eternal wrath.

*v.9.* This shows the nature of the punishment upon those who obey not the gospel — destruction without end, undying death and eternal banishment from the presence of the Lord. The perpetuity of death is the opposite of the glory of Christ and the redeemed — as the one has no end, neither does the other!

*v.10.*   He will be glorified and admired of all, but he will not have this glory only for himself individually. It will be common to all believers. He shall be glorified *in them*. They are looked upon as nothing, vile and worthless now, but then they will be precious, full of dignity, when Christ shall pour forth his glory upon them (Eph. 2:7). 'You will be among that number because you believed our gospel.'

*vv.11, 12.*   'With all this in view we constantly pray for you that God will keep you from falling and grant unto you perseverance in his calling; for as the power to believe is of God, so is the sustaining power. We pray that God will fulfil his good pleasure and goodness towards you in Christ and that he will complete the work of faith which he began, so that in all things Christ may be glorified' (Phil. 1:6; 1 Peter 1:3-5).

# The spirit of Antichrist revealed

## 2 Thessalonians 2:1-17

*vv.1, 2.*   Every believer sets a high value on the return of our Lord, the resurrection of the dead and the day when we shall see Christ and be like him. But the apostle warns this early church against becoming unsettled, alarmed and excited by fanatics and false teachers who declare that the return of Christ is at hand or on a near fixed date! When any event is said to be near at hand and it does not arrive quickly, dis-

appointment gives way to despair. 'Do not be disturbed by
their claim to spiritual revelations or by their persuasive words
or even by epistles addressed to you in my name!'

*vv.3, 4.*    'Do not be deceived by any man into thinking that
the day of the Lord is near at hand' (remember that this was
written 1900 years ago in the very earliest days of the church),
'for there must come an apostasy (a falling away from the
truth of the gospel, from the grace of God in Christ, and from
salvation by grace through faith) of those who profess to know
God and to be saved! And the man of sin, the son of perdition,
must be revealed (the one who exalts himself above God,
dwelling in the house of God, claiming to be God).' Many
believe this man of sin (or Antichrist) to be an individual or
a single person. Both Calvin and Gill say it is not an individual
but a succession of religious leaders, or a spirit of Antichrist.
Both Gill and Calvin teach that this apostasy has occurred
and that this spirit of Antichrist certainly has possessed religion as a whole. The will of man is exalted above God in the
churches, salvation has been reduced to works and deeds,
God's sovereignty and reign over all things have been denied,
and the spirit of Antichrist reigns in most churches.

*vv.5-8.*    These verses seem to bear out the teaching of Calvin
and Gill. For Paul says, 'You know what is restraining him
from being revealed at this time (or taking over completely at
this time) that he might be revealed in his appointed time (for
that spirit of Antichrist and rebellion against God is already at
work in the world).' He is restrained by the Holy Spirit, and
when God's appointed day comes, this spirit of Antichrist will
totally dominate and the Lord Jesus will bring an end to him
and his religious kingdom when he comes again!' (1 John 2:18;
2 Tim. 3:1-7.)

*vv.9-12.*    This Antichrist spirit (false religion and righteousness of men as opposed to the righteousness of God in Christ)
is motivated and masterminded by Satan (2 Cor. 11:13-15).

It will be attended by great power, success and all sorts of pretended miracles, marvels and lying wonders (Matt. 24:24). Those who follow these teachers of false religion do so not because they have not heard or read the truth of Christ, but because they will not receive the truth. Therefore, because they will not love the truth nor receive it, God sends them strong influence and delusions, which lead them to hold even more strongly to their error. There are none so blind as those who will not see! Those who take pleasure in righteousness, even in their own self-righteousness, will reap the fruit of it.

*v.13.* Lest these believers should be discouraged and fearful of their security in Christ because of his account of the Antichrist and his followers, Paul encourages them in this verse.

1. 'I thank God for you brethren, beloved of the Lord.' It is only because of the grace of God that we do not perish with the apostates. Thank God he loved us first (1 John 4:10, 19).

2. 'God chose you from the beginning to salvation.' We were elected to salvation in Christ before the foundation of the world (Eph. 1:3-6).

3. 'Through sanctification of the Spirit and belief of the gospel.' Election is not salvation, but *unto* salvation. Those elected must be regenerated, born again, called by the Holy Spirit to genuine repentance towards God and faith in the Lord Jesus. The Holy Spirit is the agent and the Word of God is the seed, instrument or foundation of faith. There is a three-fold sanctification of the believer: (1) set apart by the Father (Jude 1), (2) made holy and unblameable by Christ (1 Cor. 1:2), and (3) regenerated and progressively sanctified by the Spirit and the Word (2 Thess. 2:13).

*v.14.* It is by and through the gospel that men are called to obtain and share in the glory of our Lord Jesus Christ (Rom. 10:13-15).

*vv.15-17.* 'So, brethren, stand firm in the faith and hold fast to the truth which you have been taught through our messages and epistles. And may God comfort you, encourage your hearts and make you steadfast in every good work and word!'

# Proficient in two things

## 2 Thessalonians 3:1-5

*v.1.* **'Brethren, pray for us.'** The apostle Paul was himself a man of prayer. Evidently he surpassed all others in earnestness of prayer; nevertheless, frequently he requested all believers to pray for him and for all ministers of the gospel (1 Thess. 5:25; Heb. 13:18).

His concern is not so much for himself or the safety and welfare of the ministers themselves, but for the advancement and glory of the gospel of Christ. We should pray for the general health, gifts, wisdom, perseverance and safety of those who minister the gospel to us. But in prayer to God our chief concern is (1) that **'the Word of the Lord'** may be spread far and wide, (2) that doors may be opened in many places for the preaching of Christ (Col. 4:3), and (3) that the gospel may **'be glorified'** or triumph in other places, as it has in you. The gospel is glorified when men believe it, receive it and walk in holiness before God.

*v.2.* Pray that true ministers of the gospel may be delivered (1) from religious Jews who, with a mad zeal of law and works, do strongly persecute the gospel and those who preach it (Rom. 15:30, 31), and (2) from false brethren in the church, who go by the name of Christ but who are in reality enemies of the gospel, tares among the wheat, and have their own designs in mind rather than the glory of Christ (2 Peter 2:1; 1 Tim. 4:1-3).

All church members, preachers and teachers do not have saving faith. They have a profession of faith, a form of godliness and the appearance of righteousness, but it is not the faith of Christ, which is the gift of God, nor the faith of God's elect, which is the operation of the Holy Spirit (1 John 2:18; 4:1).

*v.3.* This is said for the comfort of the believers, who might be disturbed by these words of Paul. When Paul writes of the subtlety of Satan, the presence of false teachers, the fact that all who profess to know Christ do not have true faith and the mystery of iniquity that is already at work, some may be troubled in mind and fearful of their own state. Paul is quick to add, '**God, who is faithful**' (to his purpose, to his promises and to his elect) will not allow any true believer to be deceived, taken in by false doctrine, overcome by Satan, or fall away. He will '**stablish you and keep you**' from the Evil One!

*v.4.* The confidence which Paul had concerning these believers was not in their strength, wisdom and good behaviour, but in the Lord – in his grace in and towards them, in the power of his might, without whom they could do nothing. Through his enabling and strengthening them, they could do all things (Phil. 4:13).

'You will continue to walk in the faith of Christ and will do those things we taught and commanded you to obey.' Paul did not put upon them anything but by the commandment of the Lord. The false teachers bind upon their followers their own rules, laws and practices, which vary with the teacher, the age, the situation or the country in which they live. The commandments of God are the same for every believer, every generation, every country and every situation!

*v.5.* Paul states here a summary of that which is most necessary for believers. Let everyone be directed in heart (that is, in truth and sincerity) to become proficient in two things: *love for God* and *patient waiting for Christ's return.*

If our hearts are directed towards love for God and a desire for the return of Christ, other things will fall into place.

1. If we have a heart love for God, we will love all others. We will seek God's glory and the good of others. Christ said the whole law rests on this and is fulfilled in this. This principle of love will overcome all adversaries and adversities.

2. Waiting for Christ will put the world in its proper place. We are not citizens of this world system, but we wait for our King and his kingdom. It will help us to endure the temporary trials and reproaches of men. It will give us comfort and joy and peace in waiting for ultimate redemption.


# A warning to those who will not work

## 2 Thessalonians 3:6-18


In verses 6-12 Paul deals with a particular fault and problem that had arisen in the church. There were some people who were lazy, living idle lives, would not work at a trade and were simply living off the welfare and labour of others. This, Paul said, is a disorderly walk and is not to be permitted or encouraged.

*v.6.* **'We command you in the name of the Lord Jesus.'** This is a delicate subject. All believers are sympathetic towards those in need and are generous with their earthly goods and reluctant to say 'No' to any who are needy or hungry. But this command is of the Lord! 'If a man who is called a brother **walketh disorderly**,' this is not a man temporarily out of work or hard-pressed occasionally, but one who continues in this fashion out of laziness and choice, 'withdraw yourselves from him and him from you, for you were not instructed by us, or taught by us, to be idle or to live as beggars!'

*v.7.* Even the apostle, who had the power and right to be totally supported and cared for by the church, worked with his hands, besides labouring among them in preaching and teaching the Word (Acts 18:3; 1 Thess. 2:9). Paul was never idle nor lazy, but always busy doing what God called him and gifted him to do.

*vv.8, 9.* 'We did not eat food freely without paying for it' (Acts 20:34, 35). The ministers of Christ are to study, pray and labour in the Word (Acts 6:4). They are to live by the gospel and are to be supported by the church (1 Cor. 9:1-14). However, to set an example for these new believers and to discourage any loafing and laziness among them, Paul laboured with his hands among them. He refused to be indebted to them lest any weak brother be offended and misled.

*v.10.* He repeats what he taught them in person. 'If anyone will not work who is able to work, then do not let him share your food (turn him away from your table).'

*v.11.* Those who do not work with their minds and hands usually spend their idle time working their tongues; they are busybodies. Having nothing constructive to do, their time is spent interfering in the private lives and business of others.

*v.12.* Now as the apostle of the Lord Jesus, Paul corrects both of these faults he has dealt with.

1. He exhorts them, in the first place, to cultivate quietness, peace and repose. 'Be content with who you are, what you have and where God has placed you.'

2. 'Work and labour in honourable employment.' God has gifted every man with ability to do something (to make some contribution to the field of labour and life).

3. 'Eat your own bread which is earned by your own labour and bought with your own money. Rejoice and thank God for it, whatever it is! Be content with what you have.'

*v.13.*    A word of caution: although there are many who are undeserving and who abuse our liberality, we must not, on their account, leave off helping those who genuinely need our help. 'Do not be discouraged or weary of giving to the needy and feeding the hungry just because there are ill-mannered people who take advantage of you' (Gal. 6:9).

*vv.14, 15.*    'If anyone in the church refuses to obey what I have declared in this letter, single out that person and do not associate or keep company with him. If you humour him and pacify him in his error, you will but encourage him to continue. But if you avoid him and let him know of your displeasure, he may be ashamed and repent. However, do not consider him an enemy or reprobate, but simply admonish and warn him as a brother.'

*vv.16-18.*    Paul's conclusion and benediction upon the brethren.

# 1 TIMOTHY

# Teaching only the doctrine of Christ

## 1 Timothy 1:1-8

Timothy, to whom this epistle is written, was known for his early interest in and acquaintance with the Scriptures. His mother was a Jewess and his father a Greek, which is the reason why he was not circumcised in his infancy. Mention is made in the Second Epistle of his mother, Eunice, and his grandmother, Lois, as believers, and of his knowledge of the Scriptures from a child. Paul met him at Lystra and chose him to be his companion to assist him in the spread of the gospel. Knowing that it would be disagreeable to many Jews to hear the gospel from the lips of an uncircumcised person, Paul circumcised him, becoming all things to all men, that he might gain some. Paul sent Timothy to several places and now he was at Ephesus, where he was to abide for a while. In these epistles Paul instructs both Timothy and the church in many important matters.

*v.1.* If Paul had been writing to Timothy only, it would have been unnecessary to call attention to his apostolic office. Timothy knew that Paul was an apostle, but Paul had his eye chiefly on others who were not so ready to listen to him or did not so readily believe his words! These are the words of an apostle of Christ whose office is by the commandment of God our Saviour. No man makes himself an apostle. Paul owes his apostleship to the Father and the Son. The title **'God our Saviour'** belongs both to the Father and to the Son, for the Father loved us and gave the Son to redeem us. The Father does nothing but through the Son.

He calls Christ 'our hope'. He is not only the *author* of a good hope for salvation and eternal life, his righteousness and sacrifice are not only the *means* of a good hope, and his promise the *foundation* of a good hope, but *Christ himself is our hope!* He is our wisdom, righteousness, sanctification and redemption (1 Cor. 1:30; Col. 1:27). We do not trust a plan but a Person! We do not merely give mental assent to facts, but we receive a Person (John 1:12).

*v.2.*     Timothy was not related to Paul according to the flesh, but the relationship was spiritual. He calls him his son because of his age, because of his deep affection for him, because he instructed Timothy in the doctrine of faith and because, as a faithful son, Timothy served with Paul in the ministry of the gospel.

Here is Paul's usual salutation: 'May you have a fresh discovery of his love and free favour and an increase of grace and the gifts of his Spirit. May you have a fresh application of the pardoning mercy of God through Christ. May you have peace of heart and conscience through the blood of Christ.'

*v.3.*     Paul reminds Timothy why he was asked to remain in Ephesus. He left him there to oppose the false teachers who corrupted the doctrine of Christ. There were some teachers in this place, as in other places, who taught justification by the works of the law, but the reference is to charge these teachers that they teach nothing that was not taught by Christ and his apostles! Nothing is to be introduced as doctrine which is not according to revelation!

*v.4.*     Paul is not only condemning doctrines which are altogether false, but also those useless speculations, theories and inquiries into matters which do not edify but only turn believers aside from the gospel and the simplicity of our Lord Jesus Christ. These speculations, endless inquiries into heritage and theories concerning what is to be are but a fleshly show, do not promote either the salvation or comfort of the people and only serve to confuse and distress the mind. They only serve to raise questions, not to answer them.

*v.5.*    These false teachers boasted of having the law on their side and were teachers and guardians of the law. Paul says the law gives them no support, but rather opposes them, for the end and design, the sum and substance of the law is love to God and love to one another (Matt. 22:36-39; Gal. 5:13, 14). This love is not possible from a natural man but springs from **a pure heart** (regenerated and sanctified by the Spirit of God), from a **good or a clear conscience** (purged from dead works, void of ill feelings, vengeance and pride) and **sincere faith**. Sincere faith, with which a man really believes what he professes, always is attended with good works and love.

*v.8.*    The law is not the ceremonial law, which is disannulled, but the moral law, which is good because God is the Author of it, and it contains good and excellent things. It is good if a man uses it for the purpose for which it was designed. But if it be used to obtain life, righteousness, salvation or acceptance with God, it will only serve to condemn. A lawful use of the law for *unbelievers* is for the knowledge of sin, the conviction of sin and to shut them up to Christ. A lawful use for *believers* is to obey it in the hands of Christ from a principle of love to him! (2 Cor. 5:14, 15.)

# I obtained mercy

## 1 Timothy 1:9-14

*vv.9, 10.*    No man is righteous in himself. The righteous man here intended is the man who believes in Christ with the heart

unto righteousness and who lays hold on Christ's righteousness
by faith, in consequence of which he lives soberly, righteously
and godly, though not without sin! The law of God does not
lie as a weight and burden on him. (1) He delights in the law
of God and God's commandments are not grievous to him;
(2) nor do its curse and penalty lie on him as a punishment to
be borne; (3) nor is it to him a terrifying law, bringing him
into bondage and fear; (4) nor is it a despised law, forcing him
into a way of life he detests. But the law is enacted for the
ungodly, the evil and the profane, for it is against such persons
and their deeds as an accusing, condemning and terrifying law.
Locks on doors are not made for honest men, but for crooks.
'Do not steal, kill, lie, etc.' are not rules needed by righteous
men, but laws enacted to control and convict ungodly men.

'**Anything that is contrary to the doctrine of Christ**' — the
law lies against it, takes notice of it and condemns it. We
observe the harmony between God's law and his gospel, rightly
understood and used. What is contrary to the one is contrary
to the other. The gospel no more excuses sin than the law
does. What is repugnant to the moral law of God is also
contrary to the gospel of Christ, who said, 'I came not to
destroy the law, but to fulfil it.'

*v.11.*   The gospel with which we have been entrusted is the
**gospel of the glory of God!** Paul sharply rebukes those who
laboured to degrade the gospel, who suggest it might lead to
a life of sin, or who try to mix it with obedience to laws and
ceremonies (Rom. 11:5, 6). The gospel of Christ reveals the
glory of God's *wisdom,* his *love,* his *righteousness,* his *holiness*
and his *grace*! It is all-sufficient in this regard, and we have
been entrusted with precious treasure. We must faithfully
preach and preserve it. We do not need to hedge it about with
laws, rules and ceremonies. Righteousness is by faith, not
obedience to laws (Rom. 4:20-25).

*v.12.*   Paul, like David, was always praising and thanking the
Lord (1 Thess. 5:18; Eph. 5:20). Here he thanks the Lord

Jesus for making him a minister of the gospel. He did not take this office to and of himself, but Christ called him to it. Christ enabled him by giving him abilities, gifts, knowledge and grace. Christ counted him faithful, having made him so by his grace, for faithfulness is a necessary requisite and qualification for a gospel minister. We are not always successful, but we must be faithful! (1 Cor. 9:16.)

*v.13.* 'I obtained mercy,' though I was a blasphemer, calling Christ an impostor! I was a persecutor. Not content to blaspheme Christ, I put his people in prison and consented to their deaths. I was injurious, making havoc of the church, using force and violence to blot out the gospel! Yet, God had mercy upon me — unasked, unsought and unmerited (Eph. 2:3-8). The fact that Paul did these things in ignorance and unbelief was not the reason he obtained mercy, but he is saying that it is indeed mercy that pardons and justifies such an ignorant and unbelieving creature (Rom. 5:6-9).

*v.14.* The grace of God flowed out abundantly and beyond measure for me. God is rich and plenteous in mercy towards me. 'Where sin did overflow, grace did much more overflow.' This grace of God *towards me* was accomplished by the grace of God *in me* which begat the grace of faith and the grace of love. Instead of unbelief, I now had faith in Christ. Instead of rage and madness, I now loved Christ and his people.

Let our attention be directed to these two graces, which are inseparable! He who believes in Christ loves Christ and others. He who loves Christ with a sincere heart is certainly born of God and has saving faith.

# A faithful saying

## 1 Timothy 1:15-20

After exhorting Timothy to oppose the false teachers and
charge the Ephesians to teach 'no other doctrine than that
which was taught by Christ and the apostles', after defending
his ministry from slander and unjust accusations, declaring
that though he was a blasphemer he 'obtained mercy' and
was put into the ministry by the Lord Jesus, Paul proceeds
to give the sum and substance of his gospel: 'Christ Jesus
came into the world to save sinners.'

*v.15.* **'This is a faithful saying.'** It is a true saying, not to
be doubted, argued or debated, but to be received and
believed (1 Tim. 3:16). Men are always disputing among
themselves about how God saves sinners. They often are in
doubt about their own salvation. Wherefore, when questions
and doubts arise, let us repel them with this certain and sure
truth: 'Christ came into the world to save sinners.' He alone
is the Saviour, and the only Saviour.

This gospel is faithful to *God's law,* which is magnified and
honoured; it is faithful to *God's justice,* which is satisfied; it is
faithful to *God's promises,* and therein is the faithfulness of
Christ revealed. This gospel is **'worthy of acceptation'** by all
persons because it is the Word of God, not of man. It is
entirely true, suitable to the need of all, glorifies God (1 Tim.
1:11) and is the gospel preached from the beginning (Rom
1:1-3).

**'Christ Jesus came into the world'** (John 1:10, 14; Gal.
4:4; Isa. 7:14; 9:6). The second person of the blessed Trinity

— very God of very God, the express image of his person —
has come into this world in human flesh (Rom. 8:3; John
10:30; 14:9).

'To save sinners.' The word 'sinners' is emphatic and con-
clusive! Many who acknowledge that it is the office and work
of Christ to save have difficulty admitting that such salvation
actually belongs to sinners! The natural mind is always com-
pelled to look for some 'worthiness' in the creature! But the
message of the gospel is 'Christ lived and died and rose again
for sinners!' (Matt. 9:10-13; Rom. 5:6-10.)

'Of whom I am the chief' — the first, the greatest. Paul does
not say this out of false modesty or for vain glory, but from
a real sense of his sins, which were exceedingly sinful to him
(Acts 8:3; 9:13).

*v.16.* 'I obtained mercy' (1 Tim. 1:13). Twice Paul uses this
phrase. 'Though I was a blasphemer, a persecutor, the greatest
sinner against Christ, God had mercy on me, unasked, unsought
and unmerited. God was longsuffering towards me in the
midst of all my sins and rebellion, as he is to all his elect.' God
held out such a pattern that no one should doubt that he
would obtain pardon, provided he received Christ by faith.
Paul is an example of the patience and grace of God for the
encouragement of the faith and hope of others in Christ,
though ever so great sinners!

Upon being told by William Jay that he was encouraged by
the conversion of a certain rebel, John Newton replied, 'Since
the Lord saved *me*, I have despaired of no man living!'

*v.17.* The apostle breaks forth in a doxology of praise to
Christ for his sovereign mercy and abundant grace. He is the
*eternal* king of nature, providence and grace. His throne is
for ever, and of his kingdom and government there is no end.
He is *immortal,* for Christ is the living God, the living
Redeemer, and though he died as man, he will die no more,
but ever lives. He is *invisible,* who was so in his divine nature
till manifest in flesh. He dwells in light that is inaccessible

(1 Tim. 6:14-16). He is the only wise God (in opposition to all false deities), is wisdom itself, and is the fountain of wisdom! To him be all honour and glory for ever! (Jude 24, 25.)

*v.18.*    Paul renews the charge he gave to Timothy in verse 3, which was not only an order to charge others to teach no other doctrine than that of the gospel, but includes the charge of preaching it himself. He tells Timothy to be true to Christ, as a good soldier in the midst of a war with Satan, evil men and false teachers (2 Cor. 10:3, 4; Eph. 6:12; 1 Tim. 6:12), according to the prophecies of the Holy Spirit regarding Timothy, and also the prophecies of prophets of the church concerning him (2 Tim. 4:5-7).

*v.19.*    **'Holding faith and good conscience.'** Faith here is a general term denoting sound doctrine (1 Tim. 3:9). There are two imperatives for a preacher or teacher.
    1. He must hold to the pure truth of the gospel.
    2. He must administer that gospel with sincerity, honesty towards God and men and a holy conversation and conduct!
    Some preachers and teachers have failed in one or both, thereby making shipwreck of themselves and others. The term 'shipwreck' is appropriate, for it suggests that if we wish to arrive safely to harbour, we must continue on the course of faith and obedience and not wreck on the rocks of works, covetousness, compromise, etc. (1 Tim. 6:8-11).

*v.20.*    **'Hymenaeus'** (2 Tim. 2:17, 18) **'and Alexander'** (2 Tim. 4:14). By apostolic power Paul delivered these men into the hands of Satan as a token of God's displeasure (see 1 Cor. 5:4, 5).

# Prayer in public worship

## 1 Timothy 2:1-15

This chapter deals primarily with the public worship of the church. The two principal parts of public worship are the *ministry of the Word* and *prayer*. In chapter 1 Paul dealt with the ministry of the true gospel; now he calls on us to pray.

*v.1.*   When the church meets for prayer in the name of the Lord Jesus, we pray not only for ourselves, our families, our friends, but for 'all men,' even our enemies. We offer 'supplications' — petitions for material and spiritual needs; 'prayers' — representing the spirit of devotion and good wishes; 'intercession' — pleading on behalf of another, and 'giving of thanks' — the element that should characterize all prayer. Prayer would not be acceptable if only offered for ourselves! This is not the spirit of love and grace. Prayer is not to be made for those in hell, to whom it would be of no service, nor for those in heaven, who have no need of it, nor for those who have sinned the sin unto death (1 John 5:16), but for all sorts of men, Jew and Gentile, rich and poor, believers and unbelievers, moral and immoral. We understand from the following verses, from our Lord's prayer in John 17:9, and from 1 Timothy 1:20 that the exhortation is for us to pray for all sorts of men, of every rank, station, calling or condition.

*v.2.*   Prayer by the church is especially to be made for rulers, governors and those in places of authority in the country, for they wield great power for good or evil — they can preserve or disturb the peace of a country and they can protect or

destroy the lives and property of men! Why pray for them?
1. The Lord sets up kings or removes them (Dan. 2:20, 21).
2. He influences their actions (Prov. 21:1).

*vv.3-7.* In these verses Paul gives reasons why we should
pray for those mentioned above.

1. This is good and acceptable in the sight of our God and
Saviour, who is the Saviour of all men in the way of providence and the Saviour of the elect in the way of special grace
(1 Tim. 4:10).

2. It is the will of God that all sorts of men be saved and
come to a knowledge of Christ. Our Lord has a people in every
nation, tongue and kindred. Do you suppose the early church
prayed for Saul of Tarsus? It was God's will to save him.

3. There is but one true and living God whom, if any man is
to be saved, he must know. There is but one Mediator through
whom, if any man is to approach God for mercy, he must
come (John 14:6).

4. When the Lord Jesus died on the cross and made an
atonement for sin, this sacrifice and atonement was made for
all sorts of men, for men of all nations, for Gentiles as well as
Jews, for rich and poor (1 John 2:2).

5. The apostle is a preacher of the gospel to the Gentile as
well as to the Jew, a teacher of the Gentiles in faith and truth!

*v.8.* In this verse the apostle's instruction concerning public
prayer takes notice of men. It is the duty of all believers to
pray, but because he is speaking of public prayer in the church,
he says *men* everywhere are to pray with a forgiving, loving
spirit and in faith! '**Lifting up the hands**' was an outward
symbol of the elevation of the heart to God. '**Holy hands**'
would indicate sincerity and purity of attitude and motive
before God (Mark 11:25, 26).

*vv.9, 10.* Though women are not to conduct public worship,
pray publicly or teach in the assembly, yet they are to join
with the whole church in prayer. For public worship a woman

should be dressed in apparel which is not showy, conspicuous, suggestive or extreme, nor dress in such a way as to attract the eyes of others or lift up her own heart in pride. There should be no excessive arrangement of the hair or decoration of the body with gold, pearls and jewellery to attract attention. Women, as well as men, should realize that true beauty and adornment are not the adornment of the body but the *right ordering of the heart!*

*vv.11, 12.* Women are not to teach, preach, lead in prayer, or have a voice in the business affairs of the church. They are to be learners, not teachers, in subjection to their husbands and to the ministers of the Word (1 Cor. 14:34, 35). Women may pray, teach and instruct other women and children (Titus 2:3; Prov. 1:8).

*vv.13, 14.* The reasons the apostle gives for women being silent in the affairs of the church and the worship of the Lord are found in the original law of the relation of woman to man before God.

1. *Man's headship in creation* (1 Cor. 11:3, 8, 9; Eph. 5:23). The woman, by divine rule, is in subjection to her husband, and any attempt by her to assume the part of the head or instructor is to overturn God's order.

2. *Woman's priority in transgression.* Man was not deceived; the woman was! She confessed that the serpent beguiled her, thereby suggesting her inferiority to man in strength, knowledge and wisdom. Her subjection to the man is more greatly imposed since the Fall.

*v.15.* Nevertheless, the pain and distress put upon women in child-bearing does not hinder their souls' salvation. They shall be saved eternally if they continue in faith. God's blessings are upon women in their true sphere, that of motherhood, home life and godliness. But perhaps the reference here is to the salvation of all believers through the divine Child to be born of woman — the Lord Jesus Christ.

# The office of pastor or elder

## 1 Timothy 3:1-7

In this chapter Paul deals with the qualifications of officers
and leaders of the churches and points to the principal reason
for writing this epistle: 'That you may know how people
ought to conduct themselves in the household of God, which
is the church' (1 Tim. 3:15).

*v.1.* The apostle, having denied to women the work and
office of teaching, proceeds to observe that though this
belongs to men, yet not to every man, but to those whom the
Lord is pleased to call and equip for this ministry (Eph. 4:
11, 12; Acts 20:28; 13:2). He gives to the church some qualifications and directions in regard to men who desire the office
and indicate that God has set them apart for this ministry.
We know that the call to pastor and teacher involves much
more than a desire to do so, but it certainly begins here.

'**He desireth a good work**.' It is not a desire for an office,
a mere title of honour, and place of profit, but the man called
of God desires and delights in a laborious work. Elders are
called 'labourers together with God' (1 Cor. 3:9). It is an
excellent labour, a useful labour and an honourable labour,
but one which involves full and complete dedication.

*v.2.* '**Blameless**.' No man is entirely free from sin or blameless in the sight of God, but the meaning is that he should be
a man of excellent reputation among men, a man of honesty,
integrity and upright conduct and conversation.

'**The husband of one wife**.' It is not required that he be married (Paul was not) or that he should not have a second wife after the death of the first, but *one wife at a time!* Polygamy and divorce were prevalent at that time. The elder is to be married to one woman only!

'Vigilant' — watchful over himself and the souls of those whom he leads, alert to the wiles of Satan, the dangers of false doctrine and the leadership of the Spirit of God.

'Sober.' A better, more extensive word is temperate — in eating, drinking, hobbies and all things pertaining to the flesh.

'Of good behaviour' — modest, humble, considerate and kind.

'Given to hospitality.' The elders minister words of truth and doctrine, but they minister to *people*; therefore, they must love and be concerned for individuals. Their hearts and hands and homes must be open to all men, especially the household of faith.

'Apt to teach' — one who has considerable knowledge and is able to explain, illustrate and communicate the truth of the gospel, one who can refute error. A teacher should have the gift of public speaking.

*v.3.* 'Not given to wine.' The elder is not intemperate in the use of wine; he is not addicted to the use of it nor a follower of it.

'No striker' — either with his hands or his tongue! He is not a bully nor a harsh person, but gentle and considerate.

'Not greedy of money' (Titus 1:10, 11; 1 Tim. 6:6-10). Covetousness and greed are distasteful in any believer, but especially in a minister of the gospel.

'Patient, not a brawler, not covetous.' He must be one who can bear trials, reproaches and injuries patiently, rather than quarrel and contend with men, one who is gentle in his rebuke, reproofs and corrections of those who fail and falter; he must not be covetous of the praise and acclaim of men.

*vv.4, 5.* How can a man preside over the church, provide for it and see that everything is in its proper place and done according to the Word of God, if he does not have the courage,

will and determination to rule over his own household (his
wife, children, servants and all who are under his roof), which
is a responsibility of far less importance, much easier done and
requiring less understanding, care and thought? No man can
be what the term *'pastor'* involves if he is not in his home
what the word *'father'* involves — a good father, a kind
father, but one who is determined that God will be honoured
and served in and by his house.

*v.6.*    **'Not a novice.'** He must not be a new convert, a babe
in Christ. Time is not only necessary for the acquiring of
knowledge, wisdom and understanding, but for the subduing
of temper, pride and impulsiveness. A new convert in such an
important and honoured position is liable to be lifted up with
pride and self-importance, which was the downfall of Satan
(Isa. 14:12-15).

*v.7.*    He must have a good reputation with men outside the
church, for though they despise what we preach, we must not
give them occasion to blaspheme our gospel because of our
inconsistent and hypocritical conduct. Involvement in ques-
tionable activities and behaviour will bring reproach from
men and open the door for Satan to take advantage and tempt
us to greater sin.

These characteristics and traits ought not to be reserved
only for elders and pastors, but should be the character of
every believer!

# The office of deacon

## 1 Timothy 3:8-16

An account is given here in Scripture of the qualifications, faith, character and conduct of those who serve the church in the office of deacon. Most agree that Acts 6:1-4 had to do with deacons. When the number of believers was multiplied from 120 to over 3,000 and still increasing, the apostles found it impossible to give themselves to the ministry of the Word of God and prayer and also to care for the physical and material needs of the people. They called on the church to appoint some men over the tables: the table of the *poor*, in seeing that none want; the table of the *pastors*, in seeing to their support; the table of the *missionaries*, that they be provided for; the table of the *sick*, that their needs be met; the *table of the Lord*, by providing the bread and wine. These are to be honest men, for it is their responsibility to distribute the funds of the church. They are to be men led by the Holy Spirit and full of wisdom, that they may know how to lead the church to carry out the will of God in material matters. The reason for the office of deacon is to enable ministers to give all their time to study, prayer and preaching, and not neglect this important duty. The financial matters of the church, care of the needy, visiting of the sick and the comfort and general welfare of the people are all very important, but not as important as the ministry of the Word and prayer. When a church is very small, the pastor can be more involved with these matters, but as the church increases in size, responsibility and influences, these matters must be turned over to the deacons while the pastors study, write, preach, pray and confine their work to individual spiritual matters which require their personal attention.

*v.8.* **'Deacons should be grave'** — serious-minded, dedicated and honest. **'Not double-tongued'** — being middle persons between the pastor and people, they must not say one thing to one and something else to the other. **'Not given to wine'**, which impairs the health, dulls the mind and wastes the estate. **'Not given to greediness'** and covetousness for money and possessions — generous with their own possessions and those entrusted to them by the church.

*v.9.* Deacons must be men who know and love the gospel of Christ. Men should not be chosen as deacons simply because they are shrewd business men, prosperous or worldly wise; but they should be selected from among men who diligently love, hold to and defend the gospel of Christ with a sincere heart and conscience.

*v.10.* One would not ordain a novice to preach or pastor a church; neither should a man be given the important office of deacon who has not been around long enough to assure the church of his faith, dedication and perseverance. When a man is given this office by the church, let him apply himself to it with diligence and dedication.

*v.11.* The wife of a deacon should be a woman of respect, serious-minded, not a gossiper, but a believer who, like her husband, loves the gospel and is dedicated to the glory of Christ. Because of the close relationship between husband and wife, a rebellious, gossiping, intemperate wife would hinder the effectiveness of a deacon or a preacher. A deacon's home life is as important as the pastor's home life.

*v.12.* The deacon does not have to be a married man, but if he is married, he is to have only one wife, and his wife and children are to be in subjection to his leadership and control.

He cannot manage the affairs of the church if he is unable to manage his home.

*v.13.* Those who serve well as deacons are worthy of great honour, respect and appreciation from all. Blessed is the man who takes the office seriously and serves well as a deacon. He can stand before God, his pastor and the church with this boldness and confidence that he has given his best.

*vv.14, 15.* 'I hope to come to see you personally before long; but if I am detained, I write these things that you may know how to conduct yourself and carry on the worship and activities of the church, which is the prop and support of the truth.'

*v.16.* This verse is a summary of the great truth upon which the church is built, of which the church is the prop and support and to which pastors and deacons are dedicated. From the greatness and importance of this truth, pastors and deacons should judge their office, so that they may devote themselves to it with deeper reverence and greater care. God was manifest in the flesh (John 1:14), justified and vindicated in the Holy Spirit, seen of the angels, preached among the nations, believed on in the world and received up into glory. This is the rock upon which Christ builds his church (Matt. 16:16-18).

# True godliness

## 1 Timothy 4:1-8

*vv.1, 2.*    The Holy Spirit distinctly and clearly warns us that in these last days some professing Christians will listen to and follow evil men who profess to speak for God, but who out of covetousness and hypocrisy handle the Word of God deceitfully. They will not only *listen* to these deceivers, but will *receive* their lies and false doctrines.

This 'departure from the faith' is their effort to persuade men to worship God and seek acceptance before God by the works of the flesh (such as abstaining from certain meats, from marriage, from food on certain days and observing certain rules and days of fasting).

Men by nature are inclined towards self-righteousness and carnal worship of God and are adverse towards true spiritual worship and dependence on the righteousness and mercy of Christ. Satan takes advantage of this weakness and through his ministers gives men something to do and something to give up for salvation (John 4:22-24).

*vv.3-5.*    These are by no means the only areas where these false teachers exercise dominion over men's consciences with their laws, rules and traditions, but are examples.

They forbid people to marry (Heb. 13:4; 1 Cor. 9:3-5).

They command men to abstain from meat, or certain meat on certain days! This is all a hypocritical pretence of holiness and temperance.

Any creature which is made for food (and this is easy to be discerned by thinking men) is not to be refused on the

basis of spiritual contamination if it is received as from the
Lord with a thankful heart and a prayer of thanksgiving,
called 'blessing' the food. There is nothing in itself common
or unclean or unfit for use if received temperately and with
thanksgiving, for nothing that goes into a man defiles him
spiritually (Matt. 15:10-20).

Those who believe and know the truth of Christ (v.3) are
freed from every yoke of bondage, ceremony and invention
of men. They find their righteousness, sanctification and
redemption in him!

*v.6.* **'If you put the brethren in remembrance of these
things,'** that is, all that he has said in the preceding words:

That the end of the commandment is love for Christ and
others.

That Christ came into the world to save sinners.

That prayers should be made in the church for all sorts
of men.

That godly women are to behave in the home and church
as godly women.

That there are certain qualifications for pastors, elders
and deacons.

That God is not to be worshipped nor righteousness sought
by carnal means and foods but in Christ only.

'If you remind them of these things, you will be a good
minister of Jesus Christ, always feeding and nourishing your
own self and God's people on the truths of faith and good
teaching which you have been taught and have followed!'

*v.7.* Refuse all these traditions, outward carnal commandments and false standards of holiness as so many godless
fictions and old sentimental tales. Rather, **'exercise yourself
in inward godliness'** — internal grace such as faith, hope,
love, humility, reverence and spiritual worship of God
(Gal. 5:22).

*v.8* **'Bodily exercise is of little profit'.** Paul does not speak here of jogging, tennis, golf or the physical exercise of the muscles. He gives the name 'bodily exercise' to all outward actions such as kneeling, fasting, eating and drinking, abstaining from meat, sex, food or whatever, that are undertaken for the sake of religion or holiness.

This is necessary, for the world has always leaned to the side of worshipping God by outward services and ceremonies and seeking holiness through making certain foods, meats and actions to be evil in themselves.

**'But godliness is profitable for all things'** — that is, he who knows and loves Christ, walks with God in truth and sincerity, is a new creature in Christ and filled with the fruit of the Holy Spirit, lacks nothing. This inward godliness is health to the body and the soul; to themselves and to others, to the things of this life and of that which is to come!


# A useful ministry

## 1 Timothy 4:9-16


In the preceding verses the apostle condemns the natural tendency to seek holiness and to worship God by outward services, ceremonies, the abstaining from certain foods on certain days and the denial of certain normal human needs. Outward religious forms, exercises and duties are of little profit. Internal godliness, such as faith, love, humility, praise and thanksgiving, is profitable in all things -- spiritually, emotionally and physically.

*v.9.*   This saying is reliable and worthy of complete acceptance by everybody (1 Peter 3:10, 11; Ps. 84:11, 12).

*v.10.* With a view to this glorious truth — that Christ is our righteousness, sanctification and acceptance, that we are complete in him, that true godliness consists not in food and drink, forms and ceremonies, days and denials, but in a vital union with Christ, which produces inward spirituality and holiness — we are willing to labour and suffer reproach. We are willing to endure hardship, imprisonment, hunger, nakedness and the reproach and persecution of followers of false religions because we trust in the living God, who is the deliverer, provider and maintainer of all men. In a providential way God gives all men breath, food, blessings and common mercies, but he especially cares for his own! There is a *general providence,* which attends all mankind, and a *special providence,* which relates to the elect of God (Ps. 37:23-26; Matt. 6:31-34; 5:45). 'The word "Saviour" is not here taken in what we call its strict meaning in regard to eternal salvation, but is taken for one who delivers and protects. Thus we see that even unbelievers are protected by God. In this sense he is the Saviour of all men, not in regard to the spiritual salvation of their souls, but because he supports all his creatures. His goodness extends to the most wicked. Since God shows mercy and favour to those who are strangers, how shall it be with us who are members of his family?' (John Calvin.)

*v.11.* 'Command men to reject all fleshly, profane, unscriptural doctrines and religious exercises, and teach them to exercise themselves in inward spiritual godliness. Teach them to love Christ and one another. Teach them to trust and depend on the Lord to deliver them from trouble and to supply every need!'

*v.12.* Timothy was a very young man. Young men are sometimes honoured by God with great gifts for usefulness in the church — as Samuel, David, Solomon, Charles Spurgeon, M'Cheyne and Brainerd. They should not be shunned because of their youth when they have gifts suitable to their office and behave well in it, but they ought to be honoured and esteemed

for their work's sake. At the same time, Paul instructs
Timothy to supply by dedication, sincerity and gravity of
conduct what is lacking in age and experience. 'Be an example
to other believers in your conduct, love, faith and purity of
life.' Proper respect and honour are not demanded but earned,
and should depend in no way upon a person's age or office
but upon his consecration to Christ and his gospel.

*v.13.*      Paul was hoping that he could visit them again, but he
was unwilling for Timothy and others to be idle. **'Give attention to the reading of the Scriptures.'** How shall we teach
others if we are not taught of God? If so great a man is advised
to study, how much more do we need such advice! We study
and read for our own growth in grace and the knowledge of
Christ, but we also study in order to communicate to others
the doctrines of Christ. It might be worthwhile to note that
reading comes *before* exhortation, for the Scripture is the
foundation of all wisdom.

*v.14.*      The apostle exhorts Timothy to employ, for the
glory of God and the edification of the church, the grace
and gifts with which he is endued. That which qualifies men
for the work of the ministry is a *gift from God* and is not to
be neglected through laziness and indifference or other
employments. At his ordination the men of God prophesied
great things through his ministry.

*v.15.*      Two things are emphasized here: *meditation* and
*dedication!* Meditate upon the Scripture, spend much time
in study, prayer and personal devotion and give yourself up
wholly to the ministry of the Word. Literally throw yourself completely into the work of the gospel. Your sincerity,
ability, growth and usefulness will be evident to all.

*v.16.*      **'Take heed to yourself'** — to your attitude, conduct,
objectives, personal faith and relationship with Christ. **'Take
heed to your doctrine'** — see that you preach the truth of the

Scriptures. These two things are most important, for in so
doing you shall deliver yourself from error, from the blood of
men, from heresies of false teachers and from becoming a
castaway. You shall also be an instrument of God to the
eternal salvation of those who hear you and a means to lead
them into the truth of God concerning their behaviour and
general conduct.

# Rules for correction and care (1)

## 1 Timothy 5:1-13

*v.1.* 'Do not sharply and harshly **rebuke an older believer.**'
Paul recommends gentleness and kindness in correcting faults.
Besides, Timothy was a young man, and while older believers
are not to be spared and indulged in error or sin, they are to
be reproved and corrected *as parents.* They are to be *intreated;*
this is a kinder approach than rebuke. It is to make an earnest
appeal with respect.

Even towards younger men the preacher is to use moder-
ation and kindness in correction and deal with them *as brothers*
(2 Tim. 2:24; 1 Thess. 2:7). Erring believers are not strangers
and enemies, but brothers, whose age, office and relationship
are not to be forgotten in times of offence.

*v.2.* When older women offend and err, they are to be
reasoned and pleaded with, as children should plead with their
mothers, for these older women are mothers in Israel and are
to be treated with great tenderness and respect.

The young women are to be told their faults freely, with
the freedom of a brother towards his sister, but privately, or in
such a manner as to preserve their purity in the eyes of the

congregation. Let none, old or young, be held up for ridicule or shame, but let their failures be handled as one would the infirmities of a beloved father, brother, mother or sister. All of us are careful to protect the reputation, character and feelings of our parents, brothers and sisters. We are slow to expose, reluctant to offend and refuse to inform others of their failures, but we rather deal with them tenderly and privately. This should be even more true of our spiritual family.

*v.3.* **'Honour widows that are widows indeed.'** By the word 'honour' Paul does not mean an expression of respect, for all believers are to be respected, honoured and held in high regard. But this is the special care, maintenance and support given from the church fund to those in need. If widows are taken under the protection, support and care of the church, it should be established clearly that they are without support, that they are indeed widows without children or family to provide for them.

*v.4.* If a woman's husband is dead and she has children or grandchildren, see to it that these are first made to understand that it is their duty and natural obligation to show kindness to their parents and provide for them as their parents provided for them when they were children. This is good and acceptable in the sight of God. No believer will shift to the church his own responsibility to care for his mother.

*vv.5-7.* Paul expresses his meaning more clearly. If a woman is really alone, has no children, no support and has fixed her hope in Christ, if she continues in faith and in the fellowship of the believers, not departing from the church and the gospel, she is to be enrolled with those supported fully from the church funds.

But those ought not to be received for support who are self-indulgent, indifferent and living careless lives. If one lives like an unbeliever, it is usually safe to assume that she is an unbeliever and is not the responsibility of the church.

It is the duty of the pastor to inform the church and those who petition for help of these matters so that proper action may be taken, that none who are worthy be neglected and that none abuse the privilege.

*v.8.* If anyone fails to provide for his own relatives in need, and especially for his parents and children, he has disowned the faith of Christ by failing to accompany that profession of faith with works, and he is worse than an unbeliever, who performs his obligations in these matters (James 2:17-19).

*vv.9, 10.* Let no widow be put on full support by the church who is under sixty years of age. Those who are still young and in good health should be able to support themselves. **'Having been the wife of one man'** has to do with divorces, since remarriage after the death of one's partner is encouraged!

The widows over sixty who are enrolled for full support by the church are to be dedicated believers who have proved that dedication and faith by consecration, good works and loyalty through the years.

*vv.11, 12.* Do not hastily enrol the younger widows in this programme of support and care, for when they become restless, and their natural desires grow strong, they may marry again outside the faith, which will cause problems for them and discouragement and difficulty for those who have supported them. Also, they incur condemnation for leaving and denying the faith and their pledge to Christ.

*v.13.* Younger widows who are idle are tempted to spend their idle hours visiting among other women and talking about things they should not talk about. When the hands are idle, the tongue is usually very active.

# Rules for correction and care (2)

## 1 Timothy 5:14-25

*v.14.* '**I encourage younger women to marry**.' The apostle is still on the subject of caring for widows, so we assume that he especially means young widows. God ordained marriage for the holiness and happiness of the race (Gen. 2:18-25; 1 Cor. 7:2-5; Heb. 13:4).

It is difficult for a young widow to live with such caution that people will not find some pretext for slandering her or questioning her purity. It is better, if possible, for her to marry, but only in the Lord! (1 Cor. 7:39.)

*v.15.* Unfortunately, there are some widows who have been drawn away from the rule of Christ and the fellowship of believers to walk in their own ways, which means actually they are under the rule of Satan.

*v.16.* If there are believers in the church who have widows and needy persons in their household, let them supply the needs of these widows and not burden the church with them, that the church funds may be used to relieve those who have no one to care for them.

*v.17.* Paul had instructed the church to 'honour widows that are widows indeed', that is, to support and provide for them, but elders, pastors, missionaries, preachers and all who labour in the preaching and teaching of the Word are doubly worthy of this support and care by the church. He does not encourage the support of lazy, indifferent, professional pulpiteers, but the full support of those who perform the duties of their office well and who labour faithfully in preaching and teaching! This honour is to be understood as that outward respect shown by words and attitude and a sufficient maintenance materially.

*v.18.* This illustration comes from Deuteronomy 25:4. Whereas the ox was not muzzled when he trod out the corn, but was allowed to feed upon it, so those who labour in the gospel ought to be allowed to partake of the fruits of their labour (1 Cor. 9:13, 14). A man who labours in your service and for your benefit is worthy of your generous support (1 Cor. 9:11).

*vv.19, 20.* Do not allow your ministers, pastors and teachers to be assailed, criticized and slandered (either privately or publicly) by individuals who do not like them or what they preach. Indifferent and careless professors generally like to excuse their sins by finding fault with the preacher. If there is a legitimate complaint, either doctrinally or morally, against an elder, established by sufficient witnesses, let it be dealt with in a scriptural and brotherly way before the church, that all may walk in fear of sin and false doctrine.

*v.21.* 'I charge you to observe all these things that I have written without partiality or prejudice.' One is not to be preferred before another, but every member of the church family loved alike. Let no judgement or action be carried out in haste or disrespect, but let our dealings with one another be in love and affection.

*v.22.* Men are not to be set apart as preachers, teachers, elders or deacons in a hasty and hurried manner. Let them first be proved and let it plainly appear that they have the grace of God in them and gifts for public service bestowed upon them. Do not join with others in the ordination of unfit persons. If you cannot prevent them from these errors through serious warnings, at least keep yourself pure.

*v.23.*    Take care of your body! Use a little wine to help digestion and other disorders. It may be, as in many countries, that the water was not always healthy and pure. Nevertheless, Paul says *a little* wine in order to discourage intemperance.

*vv.24, 25.*    In the matter of discerning sin, hypocrisy, true faith, godliness and spirituality in professing Christians we are vastly handicapped, for we can only look on the outward man and our human judgement is confined to what we hear and see.

Some men's sins and faults are so open and evident that they are clearly understood by all before that great Day of Judgement, but the sin and hypocrisy of some are so well hidden that we must wait for God to expose them.

The same is true of good works! We are well aware of the good works of most, but there are many works of righteousness and love that are so secret and unrecognized by men that they will not be known until Christ comes. In that day all shall be revealed in its true light.

# Believers are good workers and good friends

## 1 Timothy 6:1-6

In this lesson Paul gives some instructions to servants or those who work for others, rebukes false teachers, advises contentment and exposes the sin of covetousness.

*v.1.*    Every believer who works for a living has someone with authority over him. This is called being 'under the yoke'. It is being under the yoke of authority or government in the service of someone, bought with their money or hired by them. Whether his master is a believer or unbeliever, kind or unkind, good-natured or peevish, the believer is to respect, honour and obey him, which includes obedience to commands, a good day's work and respect expressed in word and gesture. If professed believers are lazy, rebellious, disobedient, disrespectful or careless in their duties, unbelieving masters will say, 'Is this their religion? Is this the gospel they preach? Do their God and their doctrine teach them to rebel against authority and destroy the order that exists between man and man?' (Eph. 6:5, 6; Col. 3:22-25.)

*v.2.* The name 'brother' may be thought to constitute equality and consequently to take away authority and dominion, but Paul teaches differently. Actually, if a believer serves under or is employed by another believer, he should show even greater respect, more willing obedience, and subject himself to the authority of his brother, making the master's place of authority easier and more pleasant. Let us give thanks for faithful, beloved and believing masters who are partakers of the grace of God, and not use our spiritual relationship as an excuse for taking advantage, but a reason for better service and more dedicated labour (Philem. 15, 16).

*v.3.* Paul condemns all those who do not agree with and teach the above. Some of these false teachers despise authority and dominion (2 Peter 2:10), even encouraging disobedience to parents, masters and government. The words of Christ and the doctrines of Christ are in agreement with godliness of heart and life. The gospel is the mystery of godliness, which promotes both internal and external holiness. It leads to faith, love, humility, patience and all the duties which we owe to our fellow man (2 Cor. 5:17; Titus 2:9, 10).

*vv.4, 5.* False teachers are puffed up with pride! The gospel of grace produces a humble spirit (Eph. 3:8), but the doctrines of men (works and self-righteousness) fill the mind with pride, vanity and self-esteem!

They really '**know nothing**' of spiritual things (of the gospel of Christ) but spend their time in controversy, disputes and strife over words, laws, foolish and unanswerable questions. Their ministry produces envy and jealousy, quarrels and dissension, insults and slander and evil suspicions. The true grace of God promotes peace in the home, the church, between labour and management and in the neighbourhood (2 Tim. 2:22, 23; Rom. 14:19).

'**Withdraw yourself from these men**', who are contentious and quarrelsome, who are always disputing and galling one another, provoking men to strife, envy and anger. They are destitute of the truth of Christ and have not the Spirit of God. They suppose that religion and Christianity are a source of profit — a money-making business or a means of personal gain. They serve themselves and their selfish interests, making merchandise of you (2 Peter 2:1-3).

*v.6.*    By godliness is meant a true knowledge of God's grace in Christ Jesus which shows itself not only in the internal fruit of the Holy Spirit (such as faith, love, humility, joy, patience) and in outward acts of worship, but also in a peaceful disposition and a gracious conduct towards others. This spirit and position, with contentment (His grace is sufficient! His sacrifice is sufficient! His love and presence are sufficient! Christ is all we need!) are great and abundant gain (Matt. 11:28-30). The believer is content with his lot, his place, his duties and his gifts, for in Christ he has all things! (1 Cor. 7:20-24.)

# Godliness with contentment

## 1 Timothy 6:7-11

A person who is born of the Spirit (has a saving interest in the Lord Jesus, is an heir of God and joint-heir with Christ and is rich in faith) has God as his portion, is contented with his lot and thankful for what he has, for in Christ he has *all things* that are worth having! (Phil. 4:19; Ps. 103:1-5; 2 Cor. 12:9.)

*v.7.* This is a reason why godliness with contentment is great gain. We brought nothing with us into this world but sin, and we shall go out the same way. Earthly possessions and worldly things have no value after death, but to be forgiven of sin and made an heir of Christ is of the greatest value. As soon as a man really learns this, he ceases to be concerned about his flesh and earthly possessions and becomes dedicated to laying hold on eternal life.

*v.8.* Having food to eat, clothes to wear and a house to dwell in, we should be content (Phil. 4:11-13; Heb. 13:5, 6). The believer is rich in grace, love, joy and faith, whatever his earthly condition. We realize that the will of God has everything to do with our present state (1 Thess. 5:18).

*v.9.* Having exhorted believers to be content with what they have and to consider worldly possessions in their proper light (as only fleeting vanities), he now explains how dangerous are the desire and pursuit of these earthly riches. If God has prospered you, use it for his glory, but to set one's heart and mind on attaining worldly place, position, possessions or praise is to be covetous (which is idolatry), to question the will of God, and usually involves the neglect of spiritual exercises and puts one in the company and fellowship of evil men. This is the snare of Satan; it is a trap filled with the foolish and harmful lusts of the world, the flesh and the devil, and will finally totally consume and destroy.

*v.10.* **'For the love of money is the root of all evil.'** If we confine this only to silver and gold, we will miss the apostle's message and meaning (although greed for gold produces fraud, falsehood, cheating, hatred and almost every crime). This immoderate, insatiable desire for earthly treasure and possessions has caused some professors to depart from the fellowship of believers and from the gospel they professed, and they have suffered the terrible consequences.

Love is a heart emotion or condition and denotes a craving, desire or concern of the inward person. So that this love for money, or possessions (which I do not have in God's purpose), or position (which I do not occupy in God's will), or power (which I do not possess) is the root of all evil. This was Satan's sin (Isa. 14:12-15). Was this not Adam's sin? (Gen. 3:5, 6.) Did not the wrath of God fall on Israel in the wilderness because of their murmuring against his providence? We come back to the statement that 'Godliness with contentment is great gain!' It is not just *contentment,* for the rebellious layabout may be content in his poverty and laziness, but *godliness* with contentment!

*v.11.* 'Oh, believer, *flee* pride, covetousness and worldly ambition, which are the root and source of rebellion. Desire the sincere milk of the Word that you may grow! Covet the best gifts, starting with love! Seek the kingdom of God and his righteousness! *Follow* after the righteousness of Christ and the honour of the gospel before men. Follow after true godliness in spirit, attitude and motive before God and men. Follow after faith, love, patience and humility! What shall it profit a man if he gain the world and lose his soul? (Matt. 6:24-34.)

# Lay hold of eternal life

## 1 Timothy 6:12-21

*v.12.* '**Fight the good fight of faith.**' We have much more important business at hand than to be over-concerned with the things of this world. The life of faith is called a warfare (1 Tim. 1:18; 2 Tim. 2:3, 4). Our enemies are Satan (1 Peter 5:8; Luke 22:31), our fleshly nature (Rom. 7:23; Gal. 5:17), powers of evil (Eph. 6:12, 13) and false teachers (Matt. 24:11). The weapons of our warfare are not carnal (2 Cor. 10:3, 4), but spiritual (Eph. 6:13-16). The prize of the high calling of Christ is eternal life. Above all, '**lay hold upon it**' by *believing* it, by *receiving* it, by *enjoying* it, by *cherishing* it and by *expecting* it. We are called unto this divine life not only by the word of the gospel, but by the internal grace and power of the Spirit. Paul commends Timothy for '**witnessing a good profession**' before the apostles, the people of the church, false teachers and men of the world (Matt. 10:32-39).

*vv.13, 14.* A solemn charge is laid before Timothy, before all ministers of the gospel and before every believer to fight the good fight of faith, to lay hold of eternal life, to observe the doctrine and discipline of the church and to preach the gospel of the grace of Christ in sincerity, purity and without compromise.

1. '**Before God, who quickeneth all things,**' that is, who gives life to all creatures, who quickened us to spiritual life in Christ and who shall quicken the dead at the last day (Acts 17:24-28). Natural men, the world and all therein are nothing; we live unto God.

2. **'Before Christ Jesus,'** who is not only our Lord and Saviour but our example, in that he bore a faithful, plain and open witness to truth even in the face of unparalleled suffering, even the death of the cross (Phil. 2:5-8; 3:8; Acts 20:24). **'Till the coming of Christ.'** This shows that Paul did not design this charge for Timothy only, but for all believers. We seek not the praise, approval and honour which comes from men, but we preach, walk and live before God.

*v.15.*    The time of Christ's appearing is unknown to all but God, but it is certain. God will bring it to pass in the time appointed by him. Our Lord Jesus Christ is now, and always has been, the blessed God. He is all-sufficient, the fountain and source of all blessedness, and the only Potentate or Governor of the whole universe. He rules over the armies of heaven and over the kingdoms of men (Dan. 4:34, 35). He is King of kings and Lord of lords: he sets up kings and removes them at his pleasure (Prov. 21:1).

*v.16.*    **'Who only hath immortality.'** Angels are immortal and so are the souls of men, but they have their immortality from God. Only God has immortality of himself. **'Dwelling in that light.'** In this frail and mortal state no man can bear to see the holiness, glory and lustre of God (Exod. 33:18-20). Even the heavenly creatures cover their faces before him. We see God in Christ spiritually and savingly, and that imperfectly, but when that glorious day of resurrection comes and the mortality of human nature is removed, we shall see him as he is! (1 John 3:1, 2.)

*v.17.*    'Warn them that are well off and blessed with material wealth, influence and possessions not to be proud and lifted up because of their blessings, so as to look down on and despise the poor.' Riches are prone to produce pride. Rich men are prone to feel self-sufficient and to hold the poor in contempt. Rich men are prone to neglect prayer, become indifferent to the worship and fear of the Lord and to rest in the security of their position and possessions. This is folly. A fool may be rich and a wise man poor, for God in his purpose and providence is the one who gives us all that we have to enjoy and can remove it as easily as he gave it! (1 Sam. 2:6-8; 1 Cor. 4:7.)

*vv.18, 19.* Much is required of those to whom much is given, for which they are accountable! True riches lie in the exercise and the fruits of grace and doing good works. Be ready to distribute and willing to give for the glory of God and the good of others!

Doing good works, sharing with others and being kind to the poor cannot lay a foundation for salvation, life and eternal happiness, for Christ alone is our sure, tried and lasting foundation (1 Cor. 3:11). But a man's attitude towards others, his attitude towards material and spiritual things and his general conduct in regard to love, generosity, kindness and good works will certainly reveal whether he has Christ as his foundation and whether he has laid hold of eternal life (James 2:14-17; Matt. 25:41-46).

*vv.20, 21.* 'Keep that which is committed to thy trust,' which is the gospel (1 Tim. 1:11; 1 Thess. 2:4). Keep it pure and incorrupt, faithfully preach it and be not moved away from the gospel by vain debates and babblings about the law, circumcision, prophecy or new doctrines which ought not to be introduced. The false teachers boast of their scientific knowledge and oppose the Scriptures. Avoid them, for some pretending to be masters of science and knowledge have departed from the faith of Christ! (Titus 3:9.)

# 2 TIMOTHY

# Stir up the gift of God

## 2 Timothy 1:1-7

This epistle, addressed to Timothy, was written by Paul when he was a prisoner at Rome. It appears that it was written a short time before his death, although some believe that Philippians, Colossians and Philemon came later, since it appears that Timothy did come to him at Rome and is joined with him in those epistles. The design of the letter is to stir up Timothy to the faithful discharge of his ministry, to encourage him to suffer patiently and to warn him against false teachers who had already risen and would afterwards arise.

*v.1.* **'Paul, an apostle of Jesus Christ.'** This epistle, like all others, is not intended for Timothy alone, but for all believers. Timothy knew that Paul was an apostle! But for the sake of others who would read these words, Paul lays claim to the authority which belongs to his special office.

**'By the will of God.'** He was an apostle not by the will of men, nor by his own will, nor by any personal merit, but God separated Paul to this office by his own will and purpose! (Eph. 1:11, 12; Acts 9:15; Luke 6:13.)

**'According to the promise of life'.** God, from the beginning, promised life in Christ; so now he appointed the apostle and other ministers to proclaim that promise and to point men to Christ, that in him they might have life (1 John 5:11, 12).

*v.2.* Timothy was not Paul's natural son, but because of his youth, because Paul was his teacher in the doctrines of the gospel, because Paul had great affection for him and because the apostles often referred to believers as their children (Gal. 4:19; 1 John 2:1; 3 John 4), Paul calls Timothy his beloved son and desires for him grace, mercy and peace from the Lord.

*v.3.* 'I serve and worship the Lord God in the spirit of my forefathers (Abraham, Isaac and Jacob), or as they did, with **a clear conscience.**' Paul was not claiming to be without sin or to have a conscience always pure, but, being sprinkled and purged by the blood of Christ, he was without sin before God. Also because he loved Christ, sought only his glory and preached truth *in sincerity* for the eternal good of his hearers (not for personal gain and honour), his conscience was clear before men (Heb. 10:22; Rom. 9:1, 2).

'I give thanks to God that I am ever mindful of you, that God has laid you on my heart at all times to pray for you.' This is a good sign, both for Paul and Timothy: for *Timothy,* in that God must have his special grace on Timothy, and for *Paul,* in that prayer for others is a mark of grace in one's soul. Men of God are always men of prayer! When Paul thought of Timothy, he gave thanks for him and prayed for him. Both are marks of real friendship' (1 Sam. 12:23; Phil. 4:6; 1 Thess. 5:17, 18).

*vv.4, 5.* When Paul left Timothy at Ephesus because of the work he had to do, there was great sadness and many tears (Acts 20:36-38). But now Timothy had served that purpose, and Paul desired him to come to Rome because he needed him there and the sight of Timothy would fill him with great joy.

'**I remember the genuine and sincere faith that is in you which was also in your mother, Eunice.**' This was rich family mercy, deserving special notice and thanksgiving that God should be so gracious to the house of Timothy. Paul designs it as an encouragement to stir up Timothy to the exercise of that grace and gift of faith! (2 Sam. 7:18.)

*v.6.* 'This is why I would *remind* you (for this cause I advise you) to exercise your gifts, fan the flame and keep burning the gift of God given to you for the ministry of the Word when God instructed me to lay hands upon you.' The more abundantly we have received the grace of God, the more attentive we ought to be to exercising it and making progress day by day. In family mercies, in personal faith and in godly gifts Timothy was abundantly blessed. 'To whom much is given, of him much is required.'

*v. 7.* **'For God has not given us a spirit of fear,'** cowardliness and timidity to perform our work and office in a cold, lifeless and indifferent manner. We do not fear men; we do not fear persecution; we do not fear failure; we do not fear devils. But God has given his ministers the *power* of the Spirit (Luke 24:47-49) to do the work of God (Zech. 4:6). He has given them the spirit of *love* for God, Christ, his church and all men, and those who have it seek not their own welfare and ease, but rather the glory of Christ and the good of souls. He has given us a *sound mind* or self-discipline (self-control) which results in prudent conduct and behaviour under all circumstances. Being of sound mind, conviction and principles, the believer will stand fast in the faith of Christ.

# His purpose and grace in Christ

## 2 Timothy 1:8-11

*v. 8.* **'Do not be ashamed of the gospel.'** It is the testimony concerning our Lord Jesus — his person, his offices, his righteousness, his suffering for our sins, his resurrection, his intercession and his return. No preacher nor anyone who professes Christ has any reason to be ashamed before this evil world, of a gospel so great, so glorious, so true and so useful (Rom. 1:16; Luke 9:26).

'**Nor of me his prisoner**.' Paul did not consider himself a prisoner of Rome, for he had committed no crime nor broken any law, and he knew that men had no power over him, nor could they hold him any longer than his Lord willed. He was a prisoner at Rome for the sake of Christ on account of professing his name and preaching his gospel! He had no reason to be ashamed himself, and none of his friends should be ashamed of him. He was setting a noble example.

Timothy should prepare himself to endure those afflictions which come upon men for preaching and professing the gospel. The gospel of Christ is the gospel of peace; yet, through the depravity of men, it brings trouble, division and persecution. The man who shrinks from the offence of the cross will always be ashamed of the gospel.

The power and grace of God will support us in trouble and affliction. If we are called to endure anything for the gospel, our Lord will be our Deliverer. His grace is sufficient.

*v.9.*    How can we be ashamed of him who has saved us with an eternal salvation, who has called us by his Holy Spirit into his righteousness and to a participation of all his grace, who redeemed us and made us his children, not according to our works (at any time, either before or after our calling), but according to his own purpose and grace, which was given to us in Christ before the foundation of the world? The Lord God chose us in Christ, gave his beloved Son to redeem us, would not leave us in our sins, but called us to himself, accepting us in the Beloved and keeping us by his power. To be ashamed of him and his gospel would be unthinkable. To prefer the praise and comforts of the world to the praise and glory of such a gracious Lord would reveal an unregenerate heart (Rom. 8:18). Note the *sovereignty of God* in our redemption: he saved us! *He* called us! *His* purpose was fulfilled in our calling! *His* grace provided the way! All of this was freely '**given**' (not earned) '**in Christ**' before the world began (2 Thess. 2:13; Eph. 1:3, 4).

*v.10.* Salvation is *in Christ*. Since the beginning the grace, gifts, mercy and love of God for the elect have all been in Christ. First it lay hid in the heart and counsel of God, then it was revealed in the promises and prophecies, then in the types, shadows and sacrifices of the law. But now it is made manifest in the freeness and clearness of it by the appearance of Christ as our Redeemer in human flesh (Gal. 4:4, 5). Were the Old Testament believers ignorant of this grace in Christ? Certainly not! (John 5:46; 8:56; Luke 24:44; Acts 10:43.) Abraham and others placed their confidence in his appearance (Heb. 9:26-28).

'**Christ has destroyed death.**'

1. He has destroyed the law of sin and death, which is the cause of death.

2. He has destroyed Satan, who has the power of death.

3. He has taken away the sting of death for his people, and that is sin.

4. He has abolished the second death, so that it has no power over us.

'**He has brought life and immortality to light through the gospel.**' Christ was the first who rose again from the dead to an immortal life. Immortal life was brought to light (or understanding) by him. The doctrine of the resurrection was known by the Old Testament believers (Job 19:25-27), but not as clearly as it is now revealed in the gospel (1 Thess. 4:13-16; 1 John 3:2, 3), or as fully as it is revealed in the resurrection of our Lord.


*v.11.* '**I am appointed a preacher** [of this gospel] (Acts 9:15; 13:2), **an apostle of Jesus Christ, and a teacher of the Gentiles.**' His chief work was among the Gentiles (1 Tim. 2:7).

# Hold fast the pattern of sound doctrine

## 2 Timothy 1:12-18

*v.12.* 'This is why I am suffering as I am.' Hated, beaten, imprisoned and called a madman, Paul preached the gospel of Christ, and he preached it to the Gentiles as well as to the Jews! The Gentiles were stirred up against him for introducing a new religion among them to the destruction of their idolatry. The Jews were angry because he preached salvation, righteousness and resurrection in Christ, making vain their ceremonies, self-righteousness and traditions. 'Nevertheless I am not ashamed.'

Here is a definition of the faith that saves: knowledge, confidence and committal!

1. 'I know whom I have believed.' A spiritual *knowledge* of Christ is necessary to faith in him (Rom. 10:13, 14). Those who know Christ (who he is, what he did, why he did it, where he is now) believe in him, and the more they know him, the more strongly do they believe.

2. 'I am persuaded he is able.' *Confidence* in the Saviour's willingness to save and power to save is necessary to faith (Rom. 4:20, 21; Jude 24; Heb. 7:25).

3. 'I have committed unto him.' Where there has been no genuine and complete *committal* of all things to Christ, there is no true saving faith. One cannot separate faith from conduct. Committal to Christ involves our trusting him, casting ourselves upon him and leaving ourselves totally in his hands to save, sanctify and glorify! (1 Cor. 1:30.)

*v.13.* Paul knew how ready men are to depart from pure

doctrine and the gospel of God's glory and grace, so he exhorts
Timothy to hold fast (both in head and heart) to the whole-
some words and truth of the Lord Jesus Christ. The word
'form' is the pattern set by Paul and the other apostles. 'Preach
the unsearchable riches of Christ, imputed righteousness,
repentance towards God and faith in Christ as you have heard
me preach it' (Acts 20:20; Rom. 8:29-34).

**'Hold [the truth of Christ] in faith and love.'** These are the
marks of sound doctrine, and he places them both in Christ:
'In the exercise of faith, from a principle of love.' These two
graces always go together and have Christ as their object. No
man can persevere in sound doctrine unless he is endued with
true faith and genuine love.

*v.14.*    'Guard and keep (with the greatest care) the precious
and excellent gospel, which has been entrusted to you, by the
help of the Holy Spirit who dwells in you' (1 Tim. 1:11; 6:20).

The gospel is a treasure indeed: it contains the riches of
grace, the unsearchable riches of Christ, and is a trust requiring faithfulness in those who are stewards of it, who shall give
an account of their stewardship (1 Peter 4:10; Heb. 13:17).
It must be kept pure and free from traditions and mixtures
of men. Whereas the apostle knows that neither Timothy nor
any other man is sufficient for these things, he directs the
keeping of it to the power and leadership of the Holy Spirit,
who dwells in all believers.

*v.15.*    Timothy, being at Ephesus, which was in Asia, was well
aware of the apostasy and departure from the gospel in that
area (2 Tim. 4:11). We are grieved by apostasy but not discouraged; rather, seeing so many depart from the faith, we are
more determined to hold fast the gospel of substitution and
keep the treasure committed to us. Evidently Phygellus and
Hermogenes were ministers of the Word who had laboured
for a while but erred from the faith and deceived the people!

*vv.16, 17.*    The apostle prays for his friend, Onesiphorus, and for his household. I believe that we can infer that the blessings of the Lord rest not only on a devoted servant of Christ, but also on his house. The love of Christ for a faithful believer is so great that it diffuses itself over all who are connected with him. Onesiphorus was not ashamed of Paul's chains and sufferings for Christ. He not only identified himself with the afflicted apostle, but visited him and supplied him with the necessities of life, such as food, clothing and money.

*v.18.* 'Mercy of the Lord in that day.' Too many are interested in a return on their works of charity and their investments right now, in this life! This prayer deals with the real blessings of God towards true believers — the *mercy* of the Lord *in that day.* How much richer a reward awaits those who, without the expectation of earthly reward from the hand of men, are kind to the people of God, constrained only by the love of Christ! Nothing can compare with the mercy of the Lord in that day (Rom. 8:16-18).

# Endure hardships as a good soldier

## 2 Timothy 2:1-7

*v.1.* 'My son' indicates the *close relationship* between these two servants of Christ and expresses the *deep affection* Paul had for Timothy. We are members of Christ's family, and we love one another. 'Be strong,' inwardly and outwardly, in the grace of Christ. 'Be rooted and grounded in it, have a full persuasion of your interest in it, preach it boldly and defend it bravely. Oppose every error and false teacher. Grace comes from Christ alone. It is to be found only in him, and what he gives in his Son, he will maintain and strengthen by his Spirit.

The flesh is sluggish and we must frequently be aroused and encouraged (Heb. 3:13; 10:24, 25).

*v.2.* **'The things you have heard'** were the doctrines of the gospel, the mysteries of the grace of God, the walk and works of faith and justification by faith alone, apart from works of the law. This was not Paul's theology and teaching alone but was confirmed by many witnesses — Moses and the prophets, Christ Jesus our Lord and Saviour and all the other apostles and witnesses of his grace and glory! (Acts 10:43; 1 John 1:1-3.)

'**Commit [this gospel] to competent, capable and faithful men,**' men who are not only believers in Christ and have received the grace of God into their hearts, but men who will preach it boldly, declare the whole counsel of God and will not be turned aside by covetousness, fear or the praise of men. If future generations are to hear the gospel, we must pass the torch on to faithful young men who will continue the ministry of the gospel.

*v.3.* It is certain that those who believe and preach the gospel of God's grace shall suffer persecution, trial and affliction for the sake of the gospel (John 16:33; 15:18-20; 2 Tim. 3:12-14). Christ is our Captain and we are his warriors, engaged in the warfare against the forces of evil! We must expect to be attacked by the enemy and put to a stern test by our adversaries. These hardships and trials are to be borne patiently and courageously for the glory of our Lord.

*v.4.* This verse is applicable to every believer. As soon as a soldier enrols himself under a general, he leaves his affairs and thinks of nothing but war. The war is first and foremost, and the soldier must relinquish all hindrances, alliances and employments of the world that would interfere with his devotion to his general and the victory of his cause. But the main reference is to ministers of the gospel, who are gospel preachers and are not to be involved and implicated in worldly affairs, politics, secular businesses and cares (1 Cor. 9:13, 14; 2:2).

Pleasing Christ, making Christ known and honouring Christ are our chief concern.

*v.5.*    If a man competes in a sporting event, such as running, jumping or wrestling, he is not acclaimed a winner unless he competes according to the rules and finishes the required distance or time set. In the same way, no man who calls himself a Christian or a minister can expect the crown of life unless he runs the race set before him according to the Word of God, looking to Christ alone, pressing through all hardship and barriers to the end of the race (Heb. 3:6; 12:1, 2).

*v.6.*    To interpret this verse correctly we must examine and stay with the context. The farmer does not gather fruits until he has first ploughed, sowed and laboured in the field. '**The farmer must labour, before partaking of the fruits,**' is the better translation. As labourers together with Christ, we must be faithful in the preaching of the gospel, witnessing, enduring hardships and trials, and that to the end, if we are to sit down in the kingdom of heaven, take our rest and enjoy the crown of glory. All three of these illustrations (the soldier, the athlete and the farmer) are encouraging us to *faithfulness, devotion, consecration* and *perseverance* in the gospel of our Lord Jesus.

*v.7.*    '**Consider what I have said**. "Be strong in the grace of Christ; commit the truth of the gospel to faithful men; endure trials and hardship as a good soldier of Christ; persevere in the ministry according to the rules and Word of God as a soldier, runner and farmer!" **May the Lord give you an understanding of these things!**' No man has understanding of the mysteries of grace in himself; this is the gift of God (1 Cor. 2:7-10).

# Persecution for Christ's sake

## 2 Timothy 2:8-14

*v.8.* Paul had exhorted Timothy to hold fast the pattern of sound words, to be strong in the gospel of grace, to endure hardness as a good soldier and to commit the truth to faithful men who will be able to teach others. In this verse he especially mentions that part of his doctrine which was under heavy attack from Satan: **'That Jesus Christ was born of the seed of David and arose from the dead'** (1 Cor. 15:12-19). Christ, our God, really came to earth in the flesh, was truly man, was truly the Messiah and died on the cross for our sins. He arose from the dead, which not only implies that he died but that his sin-offering and sacrifice were accepted by the Father, who raised him and exalted him to his right hand, where he is our Mediator. This is the fundamental truth, of greatest import-ance to our faith, which Satan and his ministers seek to discredit (Acts 4:1, 2; 17:18, 32; 23:6; 24:14, 15). Paul calls it **'my gospel'** because he was saved by it, intrusted with it, committed to it, and so as to distinguish it from the gospel of the false teachers.

*v.9.* 'For the sake of that gospel I am suffering afflictions, put in prison and even wearing chains like a common criminal (2 Cor. 11:23-28). But the Word of God is not chained or imprisoned.' Men may be fettered and bound for the sake of the gospel, but persecution becomes the means for spreading the gospel (Phil. 1:12, 13) and encouraging others to preach it (Acts 8:1-4). When men try to extinguish the light of the gospel, it burns more brightly!

*v.10.*    There is an elect people, chosen by God and given to
Christ (John 6:37-39; 17:2, 9), for whom Christ suffered and
died. It is on their account that the gospel is sent, preached
and published in this world (John 10:24-28; Rom. 10:13, 14).
For the sake of God's elect, ministers are called and qualified,
so, whatever suffering, afflictions or reproach these ministers
are called upon to bear, they do so cheerfully if it promotes
the salvation of the Lord's church. We will go to jail to preach
to a jailer, or to the hospital to preach to a patient or to a
leper colony to preach to one of his own. Our goal is the
salvation and eternal glory of Christ and his church, so whatever we endure here is nothing (Rom. 8:18).

*v.11.*    'It is a faithful saying.' Paul uses this phrase frequently
in matters of great importance and when what he is about to
say is opposite to the feelings of the flesh. Nothing is more
opposite to the thoughts of men or the feelings of the flesh
than that we must die in order to live, or that life in the Spirit
demands *death to the flesh.* It is true that when Christ died we
died with him as our representative, and we are alive to God
for evermore. But there is a daily dying to this world, to our
flesh, to those things which interrupt our fellowship and
communion with him and a willingness even to lay down our
lives for the gospel (2 Cor. 4:7-11). As far as this world, its
glories, its relationship and its advantages are concerned, we
are dead men (Gal. 6:14).

*v.12.*    If we really love Christ, are called by his grace and
are partakers of his blessings, we shall also be called upon
to endure reproach, loss of friends, persecution and maybe
even death (John 16:33; 15:18-21; 2 Tim. 3:12). Those who
are faithful in the gospel shall enjoy gospel benefits (Matt.
10:40-42; 19:29). But if we recant, disown and deny Christ
out of the fear of men, or to win the favour of men, or to
avoid persecution for the sake of the Word, Christ shall disown
and deny us (Luke 9:26; Matt. 13:20, 21).

*v.13.* Most writers agree that the meaning is that our unbelief and denial of Christ take nothing from the Son of God or from his glory; he stands in no need of our confession. Let those deny Christ who will: he remains unchanged. Christ is not like men, who are as changeable as the wind. He will abide faithful to his covenant, to his word of promise and to his word of threatenings (Mark 16:15, 16). He cannot go contrary to his word or his nature, for that would be to deny himself, which is not possible. Gill suggests that he may be speaking of believers whose faith is sometimes quite low, but Christ is faithful to his covenant engagements for them and will not suffer them finally to fall away. He is ever the same to them in love, mercy and grace.

*v.14.* 'Tell the people of God these things that I have shown you and charge them in the presence of God that they avoid controversy over words of no profit' — useless debates over doubtful subjects, which do no good but upset and undermine the faith of the hearers.

# Rightly dividing the word of truth

## 2 Timothy 2:15-19

*v.15.* Those who study the Word to please men, to boast of their knowledge of theology and Bible mysteries or to win the applause of men are not the servants of Christ! Sometimes those who are approved of by men are disapproved of by God. There is nothing that will check a foolish eagerness for man's approval and a personal display of so-called knowledge more than remembering that we must give an account to God alone (Heb. 13:17; 2 Cor. 5:9). Therefore, we study, labour, preach and declare the gospel as in the sight of God, seeking only *his* approval!

The study and ministry of the Word is a work that requires diligence, application and sincerity, and for which no man is sufficient without the grace of God. Those who are employed in it are labourers together with God and are worthy of respect and honour. If they are faithful, bold and diligent in their study and ministry, they need not be ashamed, either before men or their Master. Those who play at preaching and are covetous of honour, applause and possessions should be ashamed now and will be in that day!

'**Rightly dividing the word of truth**' is rightly handling, skilfully teaching and correctly interpreting the Scriptures in their relation to other Scriptures (concerning Christ, his person and work, the law and the gospel) and being able to give both milk and meat to feed the babes, the young men and the elders (2 Peter 1:20, 21; Acts 10:43; Luke 24:44, 45; Acts 20:20, 27; 1 Cor. 3:2).

*v.16.* 'Be diligent in imparting to your hearers solid instructions, doctrines and teaching. Aim at edifying, not entertaining!' We are not to amaze and amuse men, but to instruct them in the things of Christ. Therefore, avoid vain, empty, useless rambling, empty talk and speculation. Those who are not content with the simplicity of the gospel turn it into profane philosophy, aiming at applause rather than the profit of the church (1 Cor. 2:1-5; 1:17-24). We do not need novelties of words, high-sounding phrases and modern criticisms; these only lead men into more ungodliness. We need the Word of our Lord preached *as it is* to men *as they are!*

*v.17.* Paul compares the errors and heresies of false teachers to gangrene. If it is not cut out, it will spread to all of the adjoining parts until it destroys the man. These false teachers and their errors are to be opposed and those infected with them are to be cut off lest they corrupt the whole church.

*v.18.*   These two persons fell from the truth and went astray
into gross error, claiming that there was no future resurrection
of the dead. Some think that they taught that there is no resurrection except spiritual resurrection or regeneration. Some
think that they taught that parents live again in their children,
but, whatever they taught, it was contrary to the Scriptures
and undermined the faith of some. These errors must be
rooted up and out! (Titus 1:13, 14; 1 Tim. 1:19, 20; 4:16.)

*v.19.*   We know too well (by experience) how much trouble
and scandal is produced by the apostasy and falling away of
those who at one time professed faith in Christ. This is especially true in the case of those who were preachers, elders,
deacons and leaders in the church. A man or woman who has
been regarded as a pillar in the church cannot depart from the
gospel without involving others in his or her ruin, especially
the weak. 'Nevertheless,' there is no reason why believers
should lose heart and be over-disturbed, although they see
people fall whom they thought to be strong.

   'The foundation of God standeth sure.' That faith (which is
the faith of God's elect) is the operation of God, is the gift
of his grace, has Christ as its author, finisher and object and
is firm and immovable as a foundation laid by God! It stands
sure, being supported by the power of God and the intercession of Christ, and cannot be overthrown by Satan, false
teachers or trials of life (Rom. 8:28-31, 38, 39).

   The seal or stamp put on the elect of God is 'The Lord
knows them.' He chose them, wrote their names in his book
and will never suffer them to perish (Phil. 4:3; 1:6; John
10:27, 28; 6:37-39).

   'Let everyone who loves and calls upon the name of Christ
in sincerity depart from iniquity' — both doctrinal and prac-
tical iniquity. We have a gospel to believe, preach and adorn.
We have a beloved Master to love, trust and glorify in our
attitude, actions and words. To call *on* his name is also to be
called *by* his name as a woman is married to a man and is
called by his name!

# A good minister of Christ Jesus

## 2 Timothy 2:20-26

*v.20.*    It grieves every believer to see those who have made a profession of faith in Christ, put on a show of piety and zeal, even preached and taught the Word, fall away from grace, the gospel and the fellowship of the saints. However, Paul's object is to show that we ought not to be amazed, unduly disturbed or think it strange that tares are mixed with wheat, dead branches are on every tree and hypocrites are present in the church.

In a palace there are pieces of furniture and articles which serve noble purposes and others which serve baser and sordid purposes. There are vessels of beauty and there are vessels of clay and wood which have no beauty! In the church there are men and women in whom the beauty and glory of Christ are seen. There are also some who do not reflect the grace of Christ, but rather bring shame and reproach upon him and the church.

*v.21.*    If a man stays away from the company, the heresies, the errors and influences of these dishonourable vessels, he can be an honourable and useful vessel, set apart by God, filled with the spirit of grace, truth and love, useful to the Master for witnessing, teaching and helping others in the household of faith. But evil communications and companions corrupt good manners! Association and fellowship with unregenerate, murmuring, indifferent trouble-makers in the church have a corrupting influence (Rom. 16:17, 18).

*v.22.* 'Flee youthful lusts.' It is true that Timothy and all young people must and will avoid the lusts of uncleanness, lasciviousness and worldliness, but, staying with the subject and context, this is not Paul's meaning. He is speaking of such evil desires as are apt to entice young ministers and leaders, as vainglory, popular applause, seeking and having pre-eminence, and becoming involved in disputes, debates and divisions. If some debate arises, problem is presented or contention appears, young men more quickly grow heated, are more easily irritated and blunder through want of experience; they are given to rashness. 'Flee this!'

'Follow after conformity to the will of God; exhibit faith, love and peace with all of the believers who call on the name of the Lord in sincerity and truth.' There are enough disturbers of the church from outside without having strife and division within!

*v.23.* Foolish and ignorant controversies over matters that do not edify the church and are not clearly resolved by the Word of God are *to be avoided!* These speculations and arguments over secret mysteries, silly trifles and unprofitable traditions only serve to foster strife and breed quarrels.

*v.24.* The servant of the Lord, especially the minister of the Word, ought not to strive and contend about words to no profit! He ought to strive for the faith of the gospel. To be quarrelsome and contentious over mere words, customs and doctrines in order to show his intelligence, mastery and piety is to defeat the very purpose of his office! He is to be kind, mild-tempered and gentle to all men, preserving the bond of peace. He must be a skilled and suitable teacher, patient and willing to bear reproach (2 Cor. 2:15-17; 3:5-7).

*v.25.* Let the minister learn to correct with courtesy and gentleness those who oppose the Word of God and, in turn oppose '**themselves**', for any man who opposes truth does so to his own ruin and unhappiness. We must be firm in the truth

yet tender in the spirit with our opponents in the hope that
God will grant them repentance and an understanding of the
Word. 'Do not build a wall so high between you and an op-
ponent that he is prevented from repenting and returning
without embarrassment and humiliation.' It is only by God's
grace that we stand.

*v.26.*      Our desire and objective in ministering the truth is that
men might 'come to themselves', as the prodigal, that they
might 'awake out of the sleep of death' and be restored to
'their right mind', Rebels are like drunken men, intoxicated
with error and taken captive by Satan to do his will. Only the
Son can make us free. Let us pray for those who will not pray
themselves (Rom. 10:1).


# Perilous times for the church

## 2 Timothy 3:1-5


*v.1.*      When the apostle speaks of **'the last days'** he means the
days following the incarnation of Christ. We have the days
from Adam to Moses, from Moses (under the law) to Christ
and from Christ's coming to the end of the world, called 'the
last days'. Some mistakenly believed that these days would be
a time of peace, holiness and obedience to God and his Word,
especially in the churches and among those who claimed to
know Christ. But Paul warns Timothy and all true believers
to expect perilous, hard and difficult times, not by reason of
outward calamities, scarcity of food and dangers from the
sword, but by reason of the wickedness of men who profess
religion! The pastors and people of God will have to contend
with legalists, false teachers, hucksters and evil and profane

men and women in the churches. This situation already prevailed during the days of the apostles and has continued, growing worse, to this day (2 Tim. 1:15; 4:10, 11, 14-16).

*vv.2-4.* He gives a description of the hypocrites, formal professors and false preachers that would arise during these last days.

1. **'Lovers of their own selves.'** This is put first because all error and vices flow from self-love. He who loves himself does not love Christ, despises others and has no concern for the glory of God nor the good of others! Self-love promotes free will and human merit and seeks honour and applause.

2. **'Covetous.'** They are lovers of money, looking for personal gain and recognition in all that they do. They are not content with the providence of God, nor with what they have, nor with where they are (Heb. 13:5).

3. **'Boasters.'** These people brag of their honour, wealth, gifts, numbers and righteousness. They are like the Pharisee of old who thanked God that he was not like other men (1 Cor. 4:7).

4. **'Proud.'** Nothing is more offensive in the sight of God than pride in the creature (Prov. 6:17; James 4:6). Someone said, 'There is pride of *race,* pride of *place* and pride of *face,* but perhaps the most offensive is pride of *grace.'*

5. **'Blasphemers.'** This has to do with thoughts and words regarding the Father, his beloved Son and the Holy Spirit, to whom all glory, worship, reverence and praise are due, in whom we live, move and have our being (both natural and spiritual), and by whom we are redeemed, kept and made heirs of eternal life. Any thought or word that renders to him any less than full glory is blasphemy.

6. **'Disobedient to parents.'** These are ones who despise authority, whether in parents, magistrates, pastors, employers or whatever authority God has ordained.

7. **'Unthankful'** — to God for what they enjoyed, ascribing all to themselves and their merit (Eph. 5:20; 1 Thess. 5:18).

8. **'Unholy'** — without fear of God, or regard to his Word, or concern for the testimony of the gospel. They live and

walk in the indulgences of the flesh both inwardly and outwardly.

9. **'Without natural affection'** to husbands, wives, children,
parents and friends. It also means leaving natural relations
between men and women (Rom. 1:26, 27).

10. **'Trucebreakers,'** or covenant breakers – loosing the
marriage bond, making void contracts, agreements and promises
both to God and men.

11. **'False accusers'** – slanderers of character, careless
gossipers and tale-bearers (1 Tim. 5:19).

12. **'Incontinent'** – not able to restrain fleshly appetites,
tempers, passions and desires, even for the glory of God;
intemperate in eating and drinking, indulging themselves
without restraint.

13. **'Fierce'** – unkind and hateful, like cornered beasts,
striking out at all in reach, wounding and bent on vengeance.

14. **'Despisers of those that are good.'** Hypocrites hate true
believers as the Pharisees hated Christ. The gospel of grace and
Christ's righteousness condemn their claims and bring out their
malice (1 John 3:11-13).

15. **'Traitors.'** They will betray secrets of others (words
spoken to them in confidence) to preserve themselves or to
gain in some way.

16. **'Heady, high-minded'** – puffed and swelled up with a
vain conceit of their intelligence, accomplishments and abilities
(1 Cor. 3:7; 2 Cor. 12:11).

17. **'Lovers of pleasure more than lovers of God.'** This comes
back to the first word – lovers of self, pleasure, sin, applause,
worldly honour, making a god of their bellies and not loving
the Lord Jesus Christ. Love for him puts all things in their
proper place!

*v.5.*    They have an external show of religion, pretending great
holiness, zeal and concern for the salvation of men and the
kingdom of God; yet in reality they deny the very heart of
true faith – **'the power of it'**! They profess the *Scriptures* to
be the Word of God, but deny the power of the Word to

quicken, to beget life and to give faith. They profess to believe
*Christ,* but deny the power and efficacy of his righteousness,
his sacrifice and his intercession. They talk of the *Holy Spirit,*
but deny his power to regenerate, to sanctify, to convict of
sin and to teach. They profess to believe *the gospel,* but deny
the power of the gospel to save, to justify, to make men new
creatures in Christ and to satisfy fully every need through
and by Christ.

# False teachers described and denounced

## 2 Timothy 3:6-11

*v.6.* The false teachers described in the verses above work
after the manner of their father, Satan. As Satan attacked the
woman and not the man (the subtle tempter beguiled Eve and
not Adam), so these, his instruments, work themselves into
the affection of the weaker vessel (1 Tim. 2:14). Every cult,
sect and free-will Arminian denomination or church is domi-
nated by women — silly, easily influenced women who like to
be told that they are religious, holy and righteous! They reject
the gospel of God's free grace and mercy for sinners in Christ,
for they are full of the sins of self-righteousness and are led
forth by a lust for new teachers, new doctrines and new heights
of personal glory. The exaltation of Mary and the effeminate
influence of Catholicism has led women to think that they are
morally good and that men are bad! (Rom. 3:10-19.)

*v.7.* Both the teachers and the captives of their humanistic
religions are always learning, driven by restless minds and
curiosity, but never able to come to a knowledge of the truth
in Christ. They learn about missions, prophecy, heaven,

standards of morality and gifts of the Spirit, but never 'how God can be just and justify the ungodly'. They reform, but never repent; they pray, but never plead for mercy; they testify, but never turn to Christ; they boast of their faithfulness to religion, but never bow to the lordship of Christ. Without apology, I declare that where women reign in religion, they ruin! (1 Tim. 2:12; 1 Cor. 14:34.)

*v.8.* We need not be surprised when adversaries rise up against our Lord to oppose his gospel of grace. Moses likewise had those who opposed him when he went to Egypt to deliver Israel. (Jannes and Jambres were the magicians put forward by Pharaoh.) Satan will use any vessel, any trick and any method to discredit the gospel. False teachers have corrupt minds with neither the glory of God nor the good of men as their goal, but are counterfeits and have no understanding of the doctrines of saving faith!

*v.9.* The false teachers may wax worse and worse in error; they may proceed to more ungodliness and deceive many, but they shall not deceive the elect (Mark 13:22, 23). They shall proceed no further than the magicians in Egypt. Though they did lying wonders, deceived the Egyptians and caused Pharaoh to harden his heart, Israel was delivered! The folly of all followers of false religions shall someday become obvious to everyone, as was that of the magicians. The destruction at the Red Sea glorified God's salvation, but it also revealed the folly of all who opposed him!

*v.10.* What follows in this verse and the next is said in opposition to the preaching, practice and principles of these false teachers. Timothy was not ignorant of Paul's *doctrine*; he received it from God, it was the doctrine of Christ, of the Scriptures, and was preached by the other apostles. Timothy knew Paul's *manner of life*: he spent his time in labour (often with his own hands), his conduct was above reproach and he was fully separated to the gospel of Christ. Timothy knew

Paul's *purpose*: it was open and manifest, not to obtain glory, applause or possessions, but that Christ might be magnified in his life and his death, and that men might be saved for the glory of God (Rom. 9:1-3; 10:1). Timothy knew Paul's *faith*, either his faith in Christ or his faithfulness in the discharge of his ministry. Timothy knew Paul's *long-suffering*, both towards the Jews who were open enemies and persecutors of the gospel and towards the weak brethren in the church whose infirmities he bore! Timothy knew Paul's *charity*, including his love to God, to Christ and to men (1 Cor. 13:1-7). Timothy knew Paul's *patience*, in bearing all indignities, reproaches and persecutions for the sake of Christ and his gospel. Paul was not moved by these but persevered with courage and boldness.

*v.11.* These incidents mentioned were not all of the afflictions and persecutions endured by Paul for preaching the gospel of Christ, but they took place in those areas where Timothy lived. He knew about them and heard about them from faithful witnesses. To the glory of God and for the encouragement of Timothy, Paul says, **'God delivered me out of them all'** (2 Cor. 1:10, 11; 2 Tim. 4:17, 18).

# The Holy Scriptures

## 2 Timothy 3:12-17

*v.12.* In the preceding verse Paul speaks of the suffering, afflictions and persecutions he had endured for preaching the gospel of Jesus Christ, and he adds, **'All that will live godly in Christ Jesus shall suffer persecution.'** There are no exceptions!

Satan, the world and especially unsaved professors of
religion hate the gospel of free grace and justification by faith
alone. Going about to establish a righteousness of their own,
they are opposed to the imputed righteousness of Christ and
count as their enemies all who preach and believe it. Those
who wish to be exempt from persecution must necessarily
denounce Christ! (John 15:18-21.) All believers shall not be
martyrs, but it is absolutely unavoidable that as soon as a
true knowledge of grace and a zeal for the person and work
of Christ are manifested by a believer, this kindles the rage
of Satan and ungodly men. By persecution, slander, murmuring or some other method, trial will come!

*v.13.*    By **'evil men'** are meant not openly profane sinners of
the world nor wicked men in general, but wicked men *under
a form of godliness,* in the pulpit and the pew, who are bent
on seducing and deceiving others to follow their false doctrine
and gospel of works (Matt. 23:15; 24:11, 24). In the last days
these religious hucksters and jugglers of truth shall wax worse
and worse, deceiving many and being further deceived themselves (2 Thess. 2:8-12). It is not because error is stronger than
truth or because Satan is more powerful than the Spirit of
God, but because natural men are more inclined to embrace
error and will embrace that which agrees with their carnal
nature (John 5:42-44).

*v.14.*    'Although wickedness prevails, false doctrine abounds
and the enemies of Christ rise up in religious circles, you continue in the doctrines of Christ, which you have learned and
have been convinced of by the Word of God! You know that
what you have received was not of men, but the gospel of
grace has God as its author!' We dare not adopt all that is
taught nor defend indiscriminately all we hear, but only that
which is according to the Scriptures (Isa. 8:19, 20).

*v.15.*    'From your childhood you have been taught the
Scriptures.' The Jews very early taught their children the

Scriptures (2 Tim. 1:5). Men are not wise of themselves but are without understanding of spiritual things (1 Cor. 2:14). But the Scriptures are able to make men wise and knowing in this respect, for they testify of Christ (John 5:39). The Holy Spirit uses the Word of God to convince of sin, to reveal Christ's person and work and to beget life and faith in the sinner (Rom. 10:17; 1 Peter 1:23; James 1:18). Wisdom to salvation lies not in the knowledge of the law, rituals and ceremonies, but true wisdom to salvation is in a spiritual knowledge of Christ, which comes from the Scriptures (Luke 24:44-48).

*v.16.* 'All Scripture,' the whole of it, both the Old Testament and New Testament, is verbally inspired by God, or God-breathed (2 Peter 1:20, 21). The Scriptures are commended by their divine authority. God used men to write his Word! These men boldly wrote what the mouth of God spoke. Whoever wishes to profit in the Scriptures must, first of all, lay down this as a sure and settled point: that the Scriptures are not the words, doctrines and writings of men only, but were dictated by the Holy Spirit!

Having settled this point we can go to the next: therefore, the Scriptures are profitable for doctrine, reproof, correction and instruction in righteousness.

'Doctrine,' for discovering, confirming and teaching all doctrine concerning God, man, redemption, eternal life and all subjects concerning our lives in every area.

'Reproof' of errors, heresies and false teachings concerning the gospel.

'Correction' of attitude, spirit and practice in believers.

'Instruction in righteousness,' in every branch of duty incumbent upon men, whether with respect to God or men, the Scriptures are a perfect rule of faith and practice.

*v.17.* That the believer may grow in grace and the knowledge of Christ and be well fitted and thoroughly equipped for every good work.

# Preach the Word

## 2 Timothy 4:1-8

*v.1.*    This is an unfortunate chapter division, for our lesson must begin with verse 16 of the preceding chapter. The word 'therefore' appropriately connects Scripture with preaching. Since *all Scripture* is God-breathed and is necessary and profitable for doctrine, reproof, correction, instruction and the growth of believers, we must '**preach the Word**'. All wisdom and understanding are contained in the Scriptures (Isa. 8:19, 20; 1 Peter 2:2). Neither ought we to learn, nor preachers to draw their instructions and doctrines, from any other source! The reading of the Scriptures is recommended, but private reading does not hinder, nor make void the ministry of pastor-teachers! (Eph. 4:11-14.)

Paul charges Timothy and every minister of Christ before God, who chose us, and before the Redeemer, who saved us and whose gospel we preach, to be diligent, faithful and true to his Word, for we shall surely give an account of our ministry when Christ comes again (Heb. 13:17; 1 Cor. 3:13). '**The quick and the dead**' are those who are alive when he comes and those who have died but will be raised (John 5:22). What does it matter what men think of us or our message? It is Christ to whom we are accountable.

*v.2.*    There is no season for preaching the Word of God; we are to be earnestly, constantly and wholly engaged in it at all times. We are to be preparing for it or performing it in all seasons. *Reprove* errors of doctrine and spirit using the Scriptures! *Rebuke* sin and error, some privately, others more publicly, according to the nature and circumstances of the offence. *Exhort* men to the duties of faith, to love one another, do good works, walk as becomes the gospel of Christ and hold fast their profession with gentleness and doctrine! Reproofs, rebukes and exhortations will utterly fail if they are not based on the Word of God and given in a spirit of humility, meekness and patience! No man is to obey because we say so, but *because God says so*. If the Word is delivered in harshness, it irritates both heart and mind. All of our exhortations, rebukes and teaching are to have one source and foundation — the Scriptures!

*v.3.* This is the reason for this solemn charge. The time will come (and has come) when people will not receive the gospel of God's grace in Christ. Self-righteous by nature, free-willers in mind, proud and boastful in spirit and lovers of pleasure more than lovers of God, they will turn their backs on the message of grace, express their indignation at it, treat it with ridicule and contempt, and gather to themselves many false preachers and teachers who preach what men want to hear, promoting doctrines of free will and the dignity of men. Those who trust their religion love to have their ears tickled with pleasant music, declarations of peace and words of praise for their works.

*v.4.* They will turn aside from hearing the truth, not being able to receive it nor to rejoice in it, and will turn to vain, empty, useless and unprofitable religious fables, ceremonies and novelties. The only remedy for this wandering is for ministers to adhere closely to the pure doctrine of Christ (2 Thess. 2:10-12).

*v.5.* The more error and false teaching prevail, the more earnestly we must labour to preach the truth. The nearer danger and division are at hand, the more diligently we must watch, keeping calm and steady, doing the work of an enthusiastic, bold witness of Christ, fully performing the duties of our ministry, seeking not our own but the things of Christ. Preach the gospel, administer the ordinances and be a true and faithful servant of Christ, and we shall not be ashamed.

*vv.6, 7.* **'I am ready to be sacrificed**, my life is ready to be poured out (as a drink offering),' which shows that Paul knew that he would be martyred (Acts 20:22-25). He did not fear death nor shrink from it, calling it his 'departure' (a removal from one place to another) (Phil. 1:21-24).

**'I have fought a good fight'** (1 Tim. 6:12). Whatever may be the opinion of the world, he declares that his fight for truth and the glory of Christ was both good and honourable.

**'I have finished my course.'** The race is over, his days and years are finished (or the course of his ministry) (Job 14:5).

**'I have kept the faith'** – his profession of faith, the doctrine of faith which was committed to his trust and his faithfulness to his hearers (Acts 20:26, 27).

*v.8.* **'A crown of righteousness.'** The happiness, glory and future state of all believers is signified by a crown, (1) on account of the glory and excellency of it; (2) in agreement with the character of saints – kings; and (3) because we are raised to sit among princes and to inherit the throne of glory.

This is called 'a crown of righteousness' because it is perfect holiness and comes to us through the righteousness of Christ. We shall be like him (1 John 3:2).

'This crown is given by God, not to me only, but to every believer.' Every believer loves him and longs for his return (2 Tim. 1:12).

# And in conclusion

## 2 Timothy 4:9-22

*v.9.* **'Make every effort to come to me soon.'** Paul knew that
the time of his death was at hand. There were many things
that Paul needed to teach young Timothy for the glory of God
and the good of the church. No matter that Timothy must
leave his place of labour for a season; what he could learn
from Paul in a short space of time would be profitable for a
long period to all the churches. Those true servants who would
labour in the gospel need to confer with older, wiser and
more experienced preachers. Time spent in learning is not
lost time!

*v.10.* Demas was a close companion and assistant to the
apostle. He is mentioned in Colossians 4:14 and Philemon 24.
We do not know that he denied Christ or totally apostatized,
for to leave Paul (who was in prison), fearing for one's own
safety or for one's physical comfort, is not necessarily to
leave Christ. However, the phrase **'having loved this present
world'** is alarming. Some believe that he came back. Let us
always be ready to restore the fallen (Gal. 6:1, 2). Crescens
and Titus had gone away also, but for good reasons and with
Paul's consent; they evidently were sent somewhere to minister.

*v.11.* The beloved physician, who wrote the book that bears
his name and the Acts of the Apostles, was a constant companion of Paul in his travels and sufferings (Col. 4:14). **'Bring
Mark with you!'** Mark was with Paul and Barnabas earlier in
their travels and parted from them, causing some differences

between Paul and Barnabas, even separating them. Now Paul was reconciled to Mark and was desirous of his company and assistance (Acts 15:36-40).

*v.12.*    Tychicus was evidently sent to Ephesus to supply the place of Timothy while he came to Rome.

*v.13.*    'Bring the cloak.' Interpreters are not agreed on this, but most believe that with winter coming on (v.21), the apostle needed his cloak for warmth. His books and parchments were especially important to him, for Paul was a diligent reader and student of the Old Testament and other books. Though he was old and near his end, yet he was mindful of his books and desirous of having them to read (2 Tim. 2:15).

*vv.14, 15.*    Alexander may be the same person mentioned in Acts 19:33, 34. Definitely he is the one in 1 Timothy 1:20. Paul said, 'He did me great wrong and the Lord will deal with him for his opposition to the gospel and to his servant.' Alexander was now at Ephesus and, since he was such a malicious blasphemer, Timothy was warned to shun him, for he resisted Paul's message strongly.

*v.16.*    At his first trial in Rome none of his friends from Judea and Asia appeared to plead his cause or to be a witness for him. Evidently they feared for their lives, as our Lord's disciples did when he was apprehended, forsaking him and fleeing. Paul loved these friends and prayed that God would forgive them (Luke 22:32).

*v.17.*    'But the Lord strengthened me.' Paul does not boast of his courage and faithfulness, but gives thanks to the Lord (Ps. 27:10). Though reduced to extremities, he does not give up nor lose heart, for he is supported by the grace and power of the Lord and is satisfied with this.

He was God's chosen vessel and instrument to preach the gospel to the Gentiles, even in Caesar's palace. Therefore, he was delivered by the power of God from the very jaws of death, from the hand of Satan and from the hand of Nero, the Roman Emperor. His deliverance was a miracle of God!

*v.18.*    He declared that he had the same hope for the future, not that he would escape death altogether, for he must die; but he could not be vanquished by Satan or turned aside from the ministry of Christ until his work was done and God's purpose for him was accomplished (Ps. 91:2-7). The believer does not trust in the flesh, nor stand by the power of men, nor fear what men can do. We are immortal until God calls us home, to whom be all the glory for ever and ever! Salvation is of the Lord from beginning to end!

*v.19.*    'Give my greeting to Priscilla and Aquila' (Acts 18:2, 3) 'and to the household of Onesiphorus' (2 Tim. 1:16-18).

*v.20.*    Erastus was a steward or official in Corinth (Rom. 16:23) who went with Timothy to Macedonia, but returned to Corinth to stay. Trophimus was an Asian of the city of Ephesus (Acts 20:4; 21:29).

*v.21.*    'Come to me before winter, when travelling will be more difficult. All the brethren here wish to be remembered to you.'

*v.22.*    'The Lord Jesus Christ be with your spirit, to counsel and advise, to comfort under every trial, to supply with all grace, to keep from every enemy and to fit you for every service. God's favour and blessings be with you! Amen.'

# BIBLE CLASS
# COMMENTARY SERIES

*by*
*Henry T. Mahan*

# Notes

# Notes

# Notes

# Notes

**Notes**

**Notes**

# Notes

**Notes**

# Notes

# Notes

# Notes

# Notes